Dear O.B.D,

This is a gratitude to life, a tribute to the divine that guides our steps. I thank God for all the blessings and, above all, for placing you in my path. I believe that the true purpose of existence is to give meaning to the lives around us, and you, dear O.B.D, are the deepest meaning of my journey.

Your love fills every empty space, brightens every shadow, and adds color to every moment. You are the reason why my life has such a special purpose. Loving you is a divine gift, and for that, I express my gratitude to God for placing you at the center of my heart.

With all my love,

David Lucas

2024

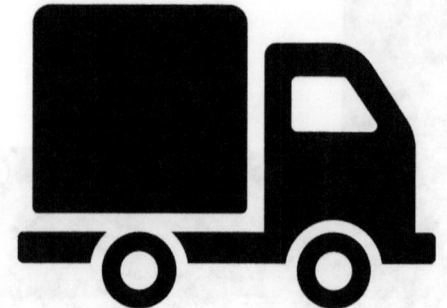

This Book Belongs to:

○————————————————————————○

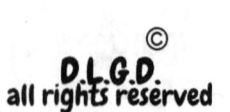

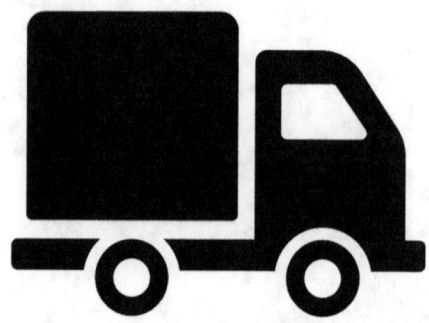

ALL RIGHTS RESERVED©
2023

No part of this publication may be reproduced, distributed, or transmitted in any form or by any means, including photocopying, recording, or other electronic or mechanical methods, without the prior written permission of the publisher, except for brief quotations incorporated in critical reviews and other specific noncommercial uses. Any unauthorized replica of this work is prohibited.

D.L.G.D.©
DLGD publications

Test Color Page

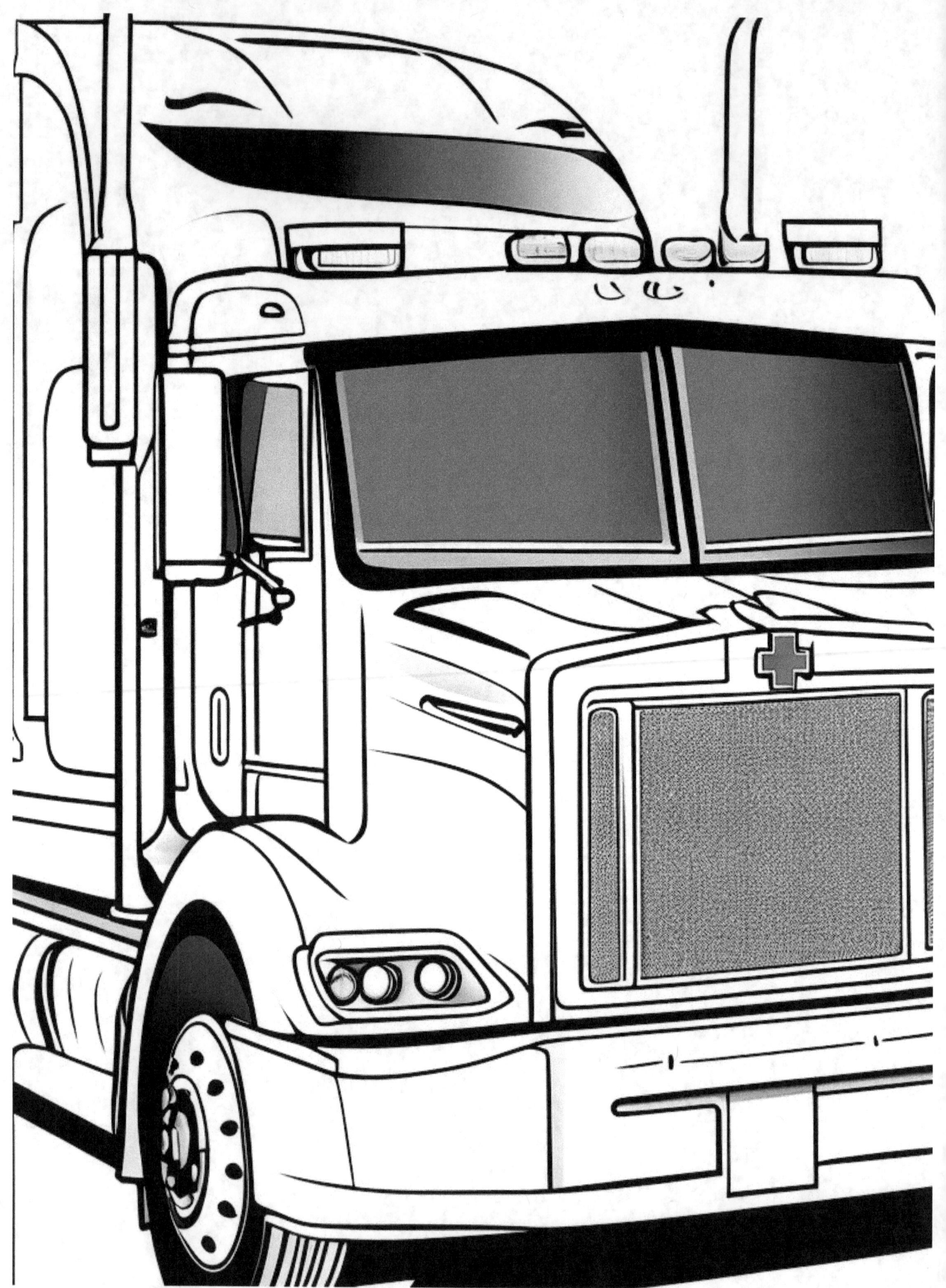

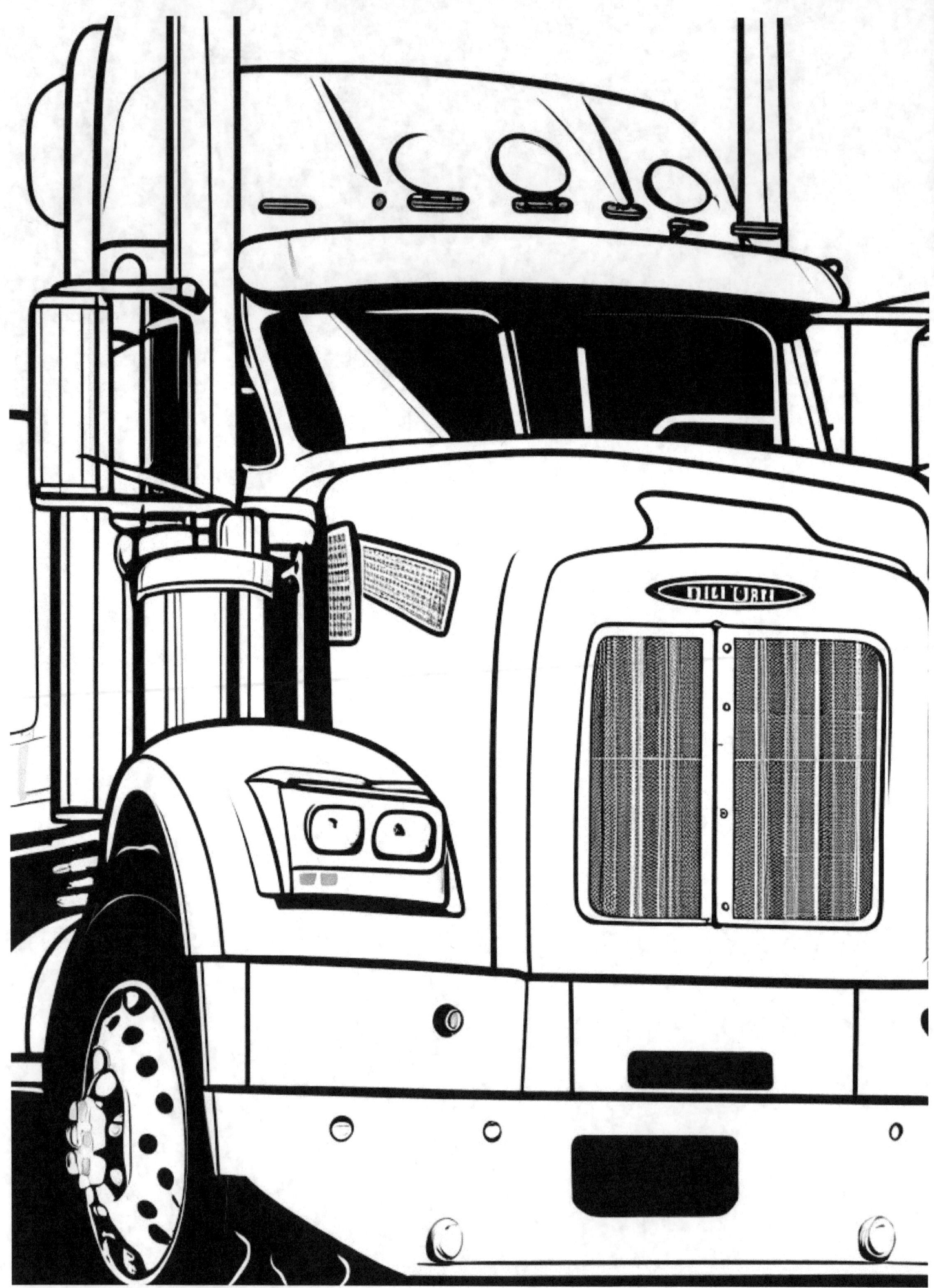

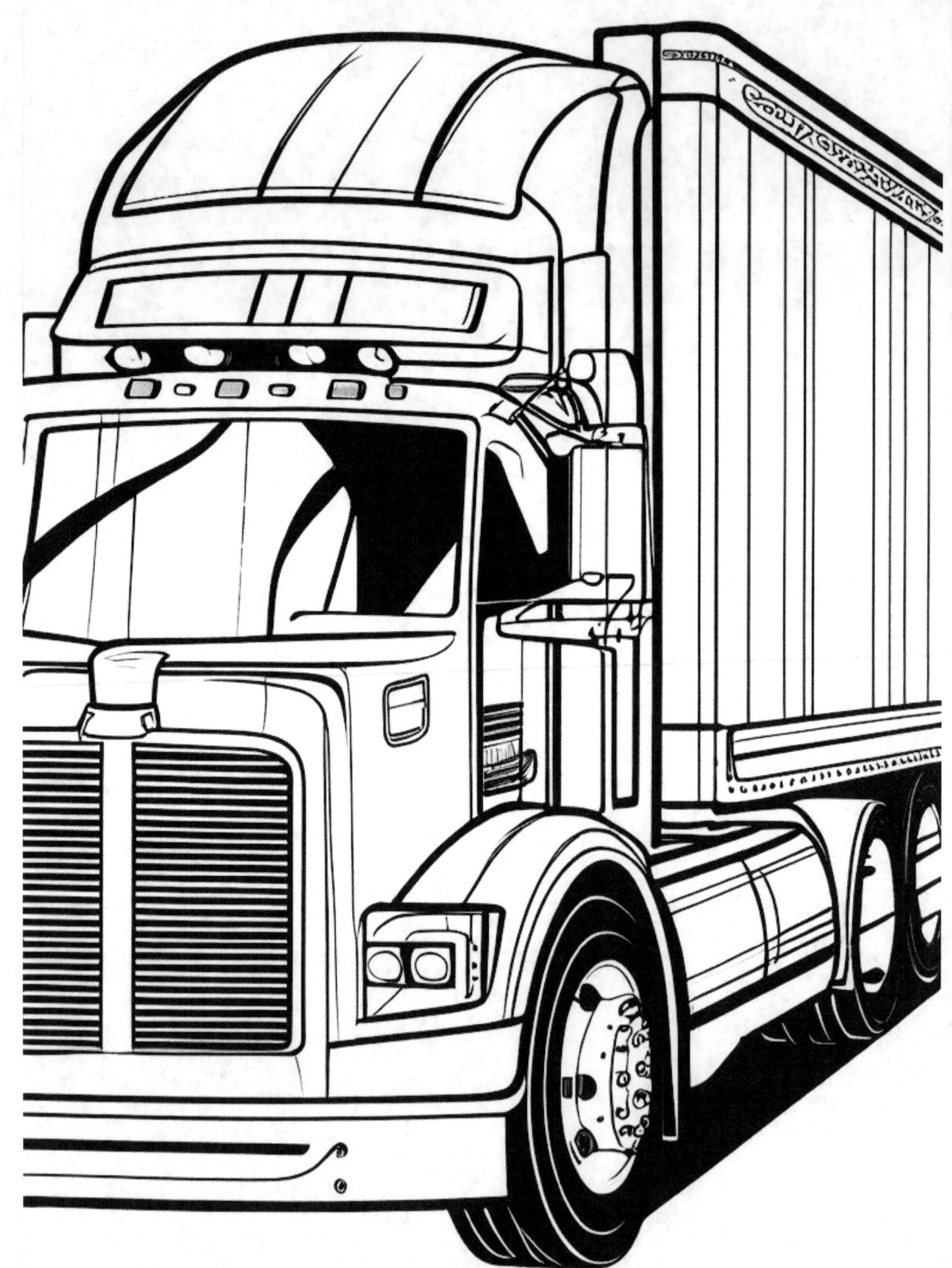

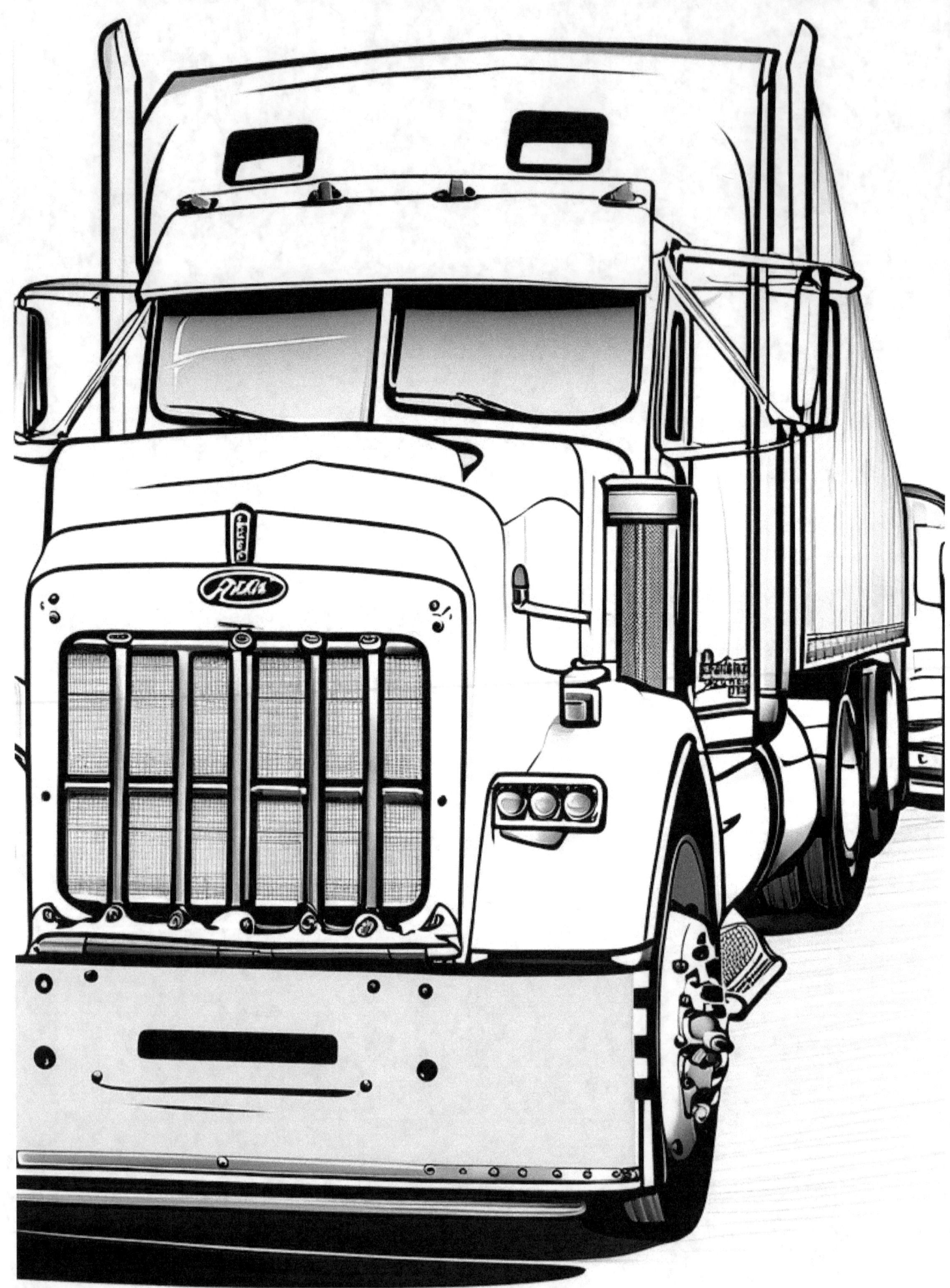

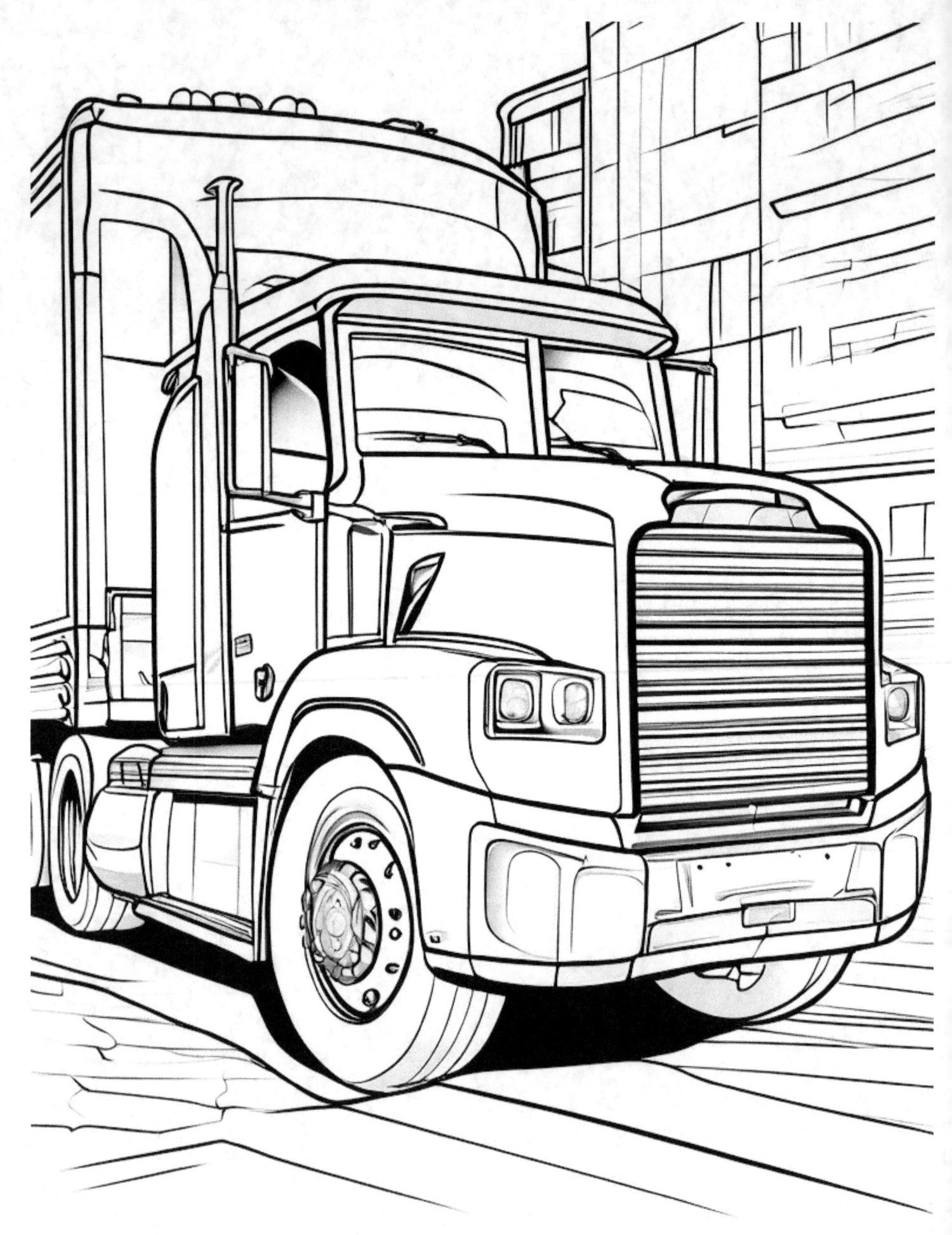

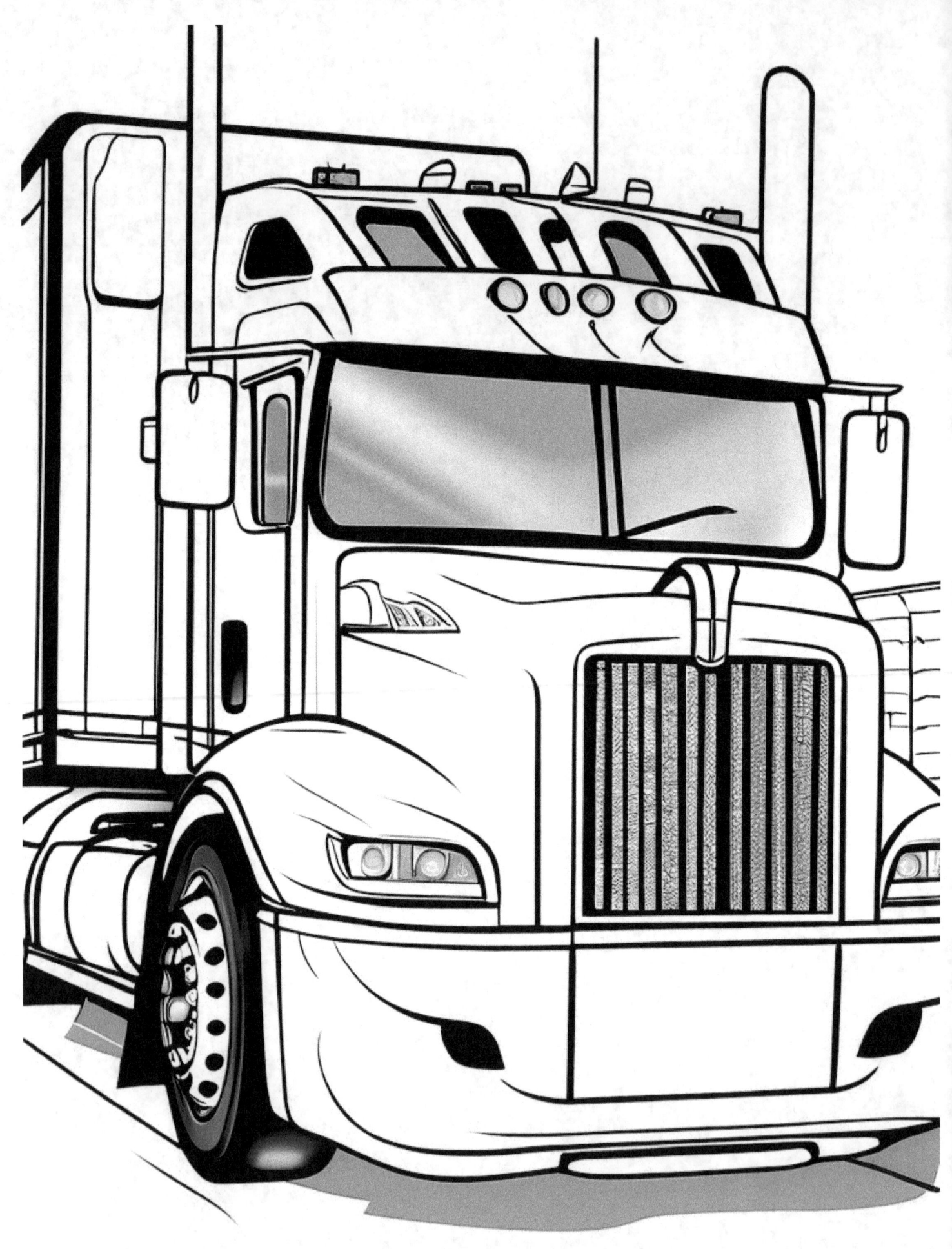

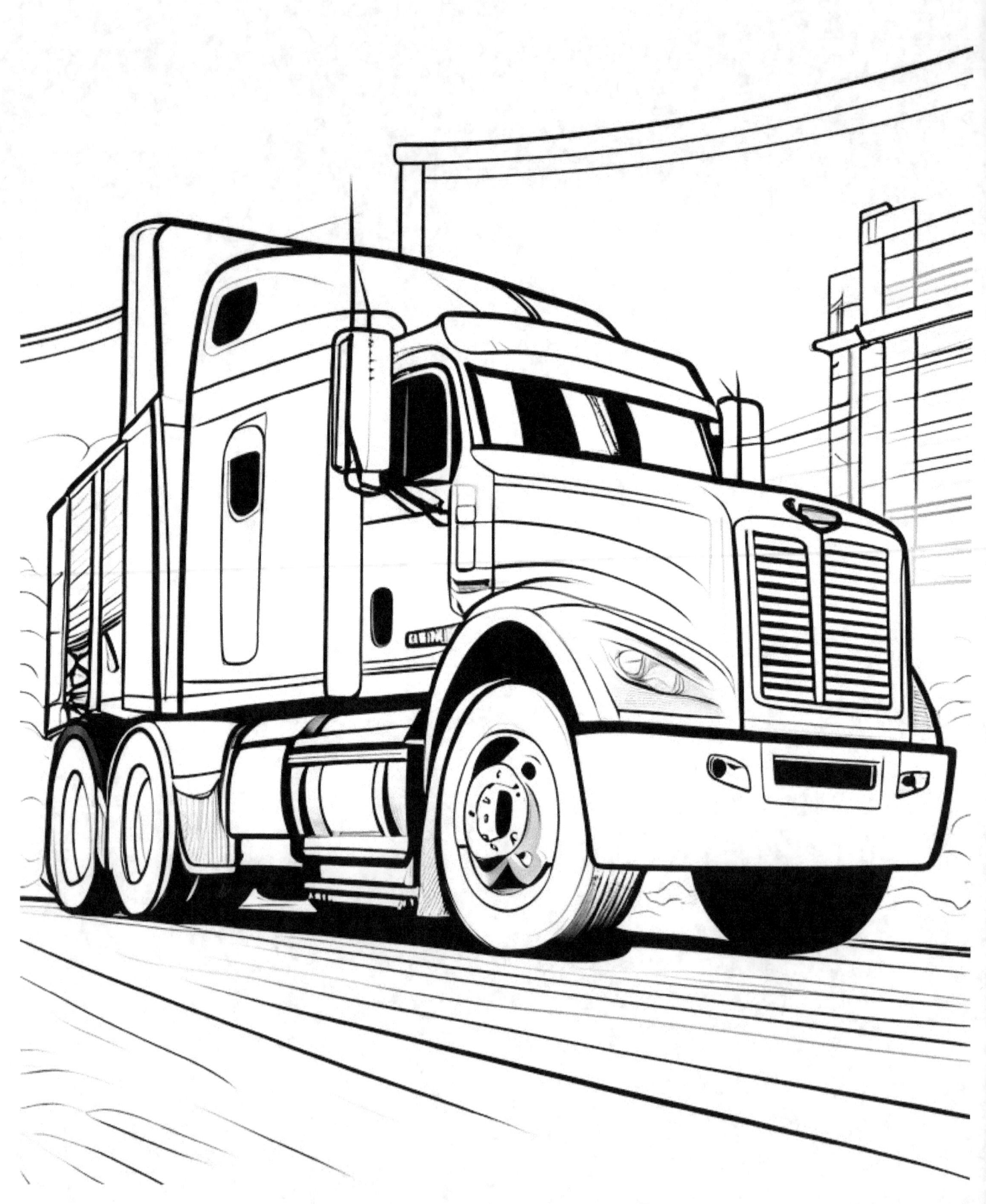

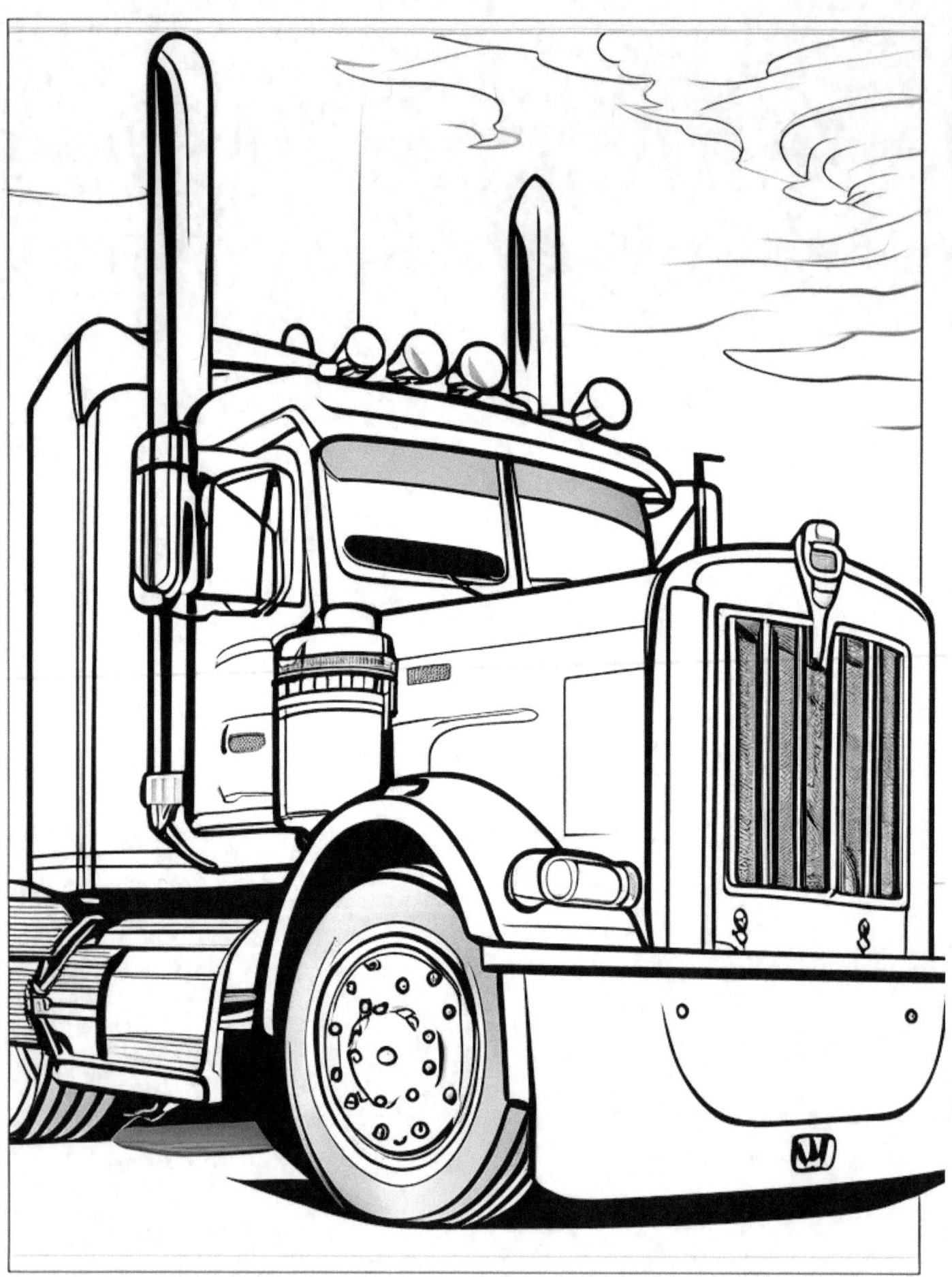

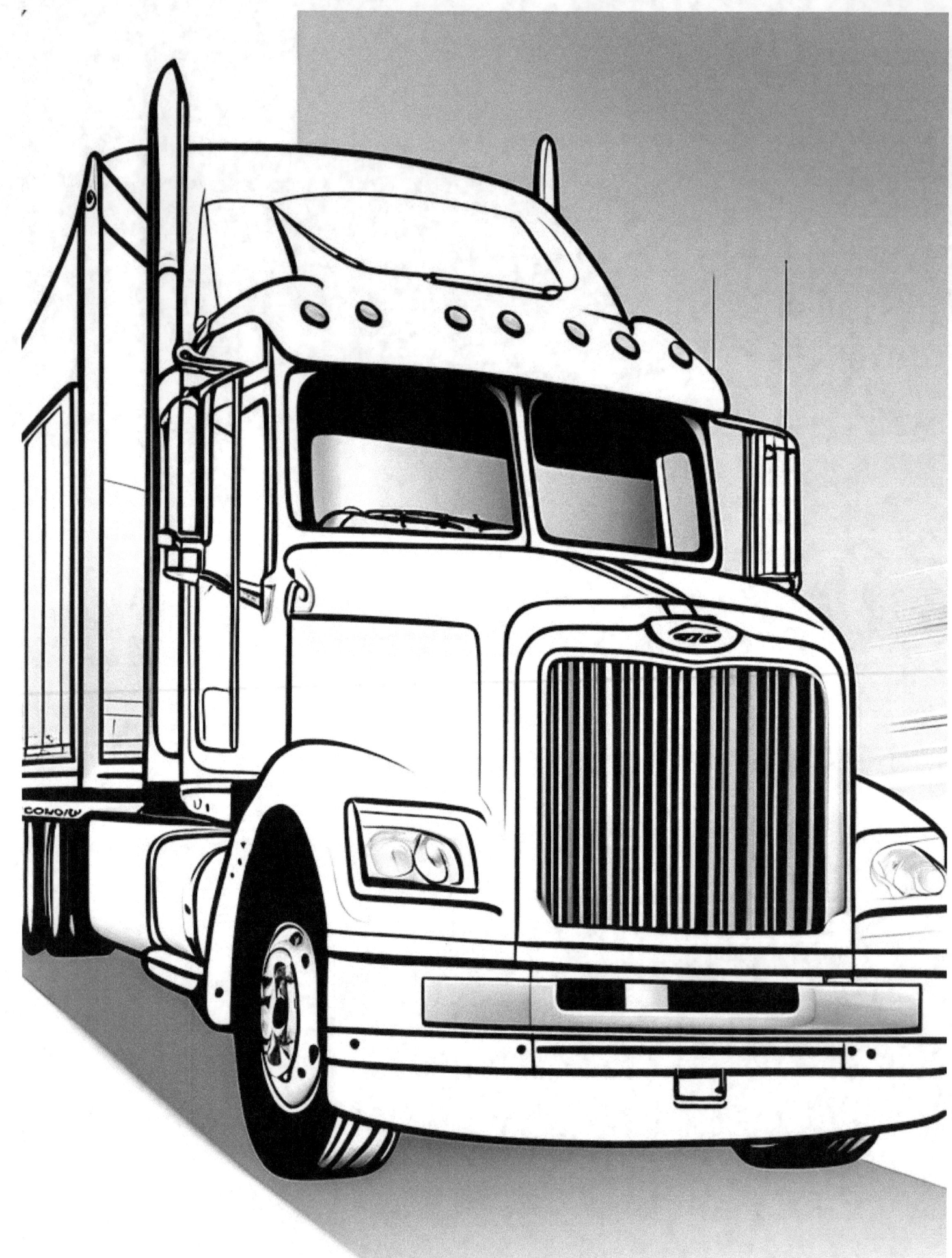

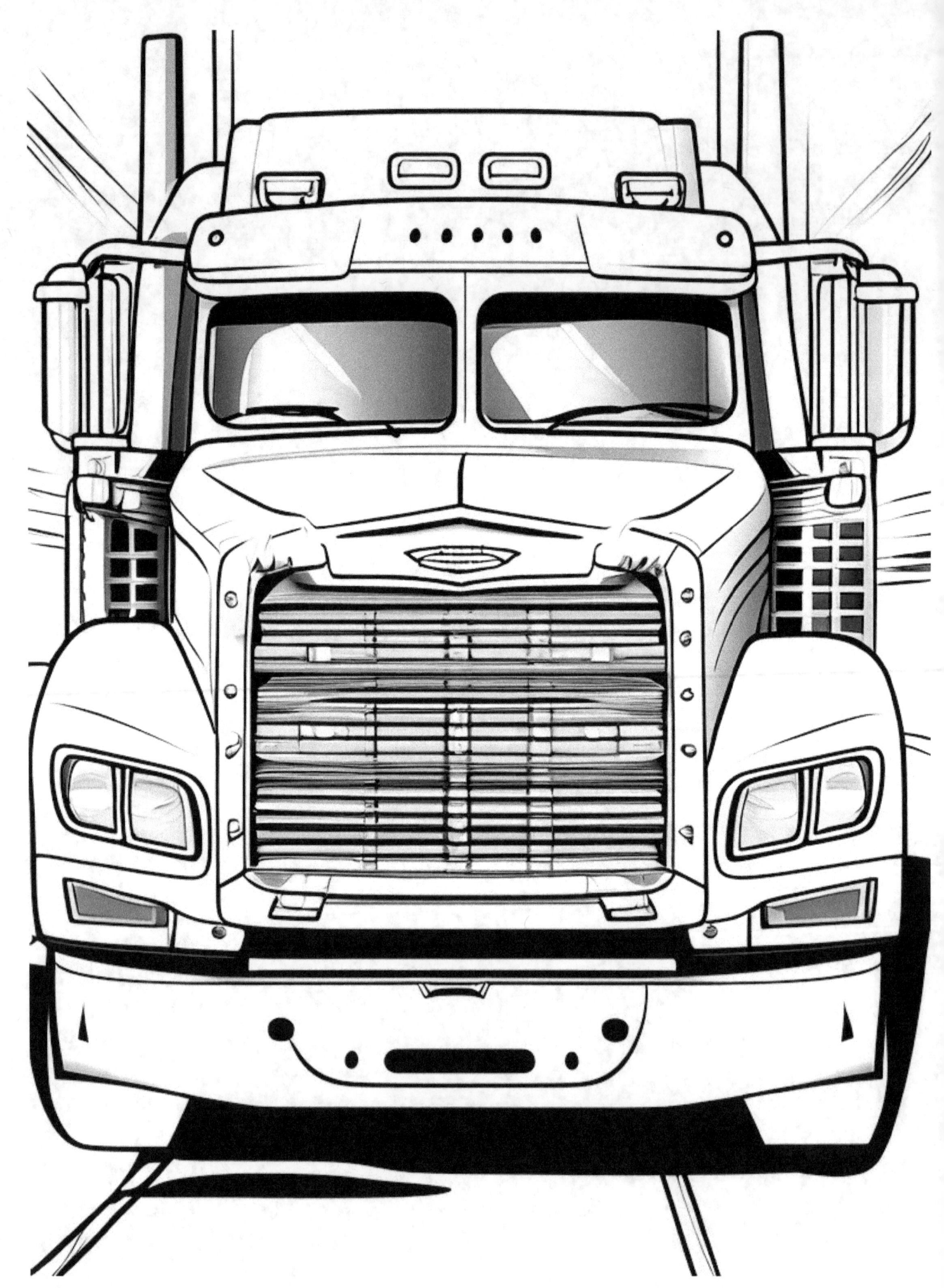

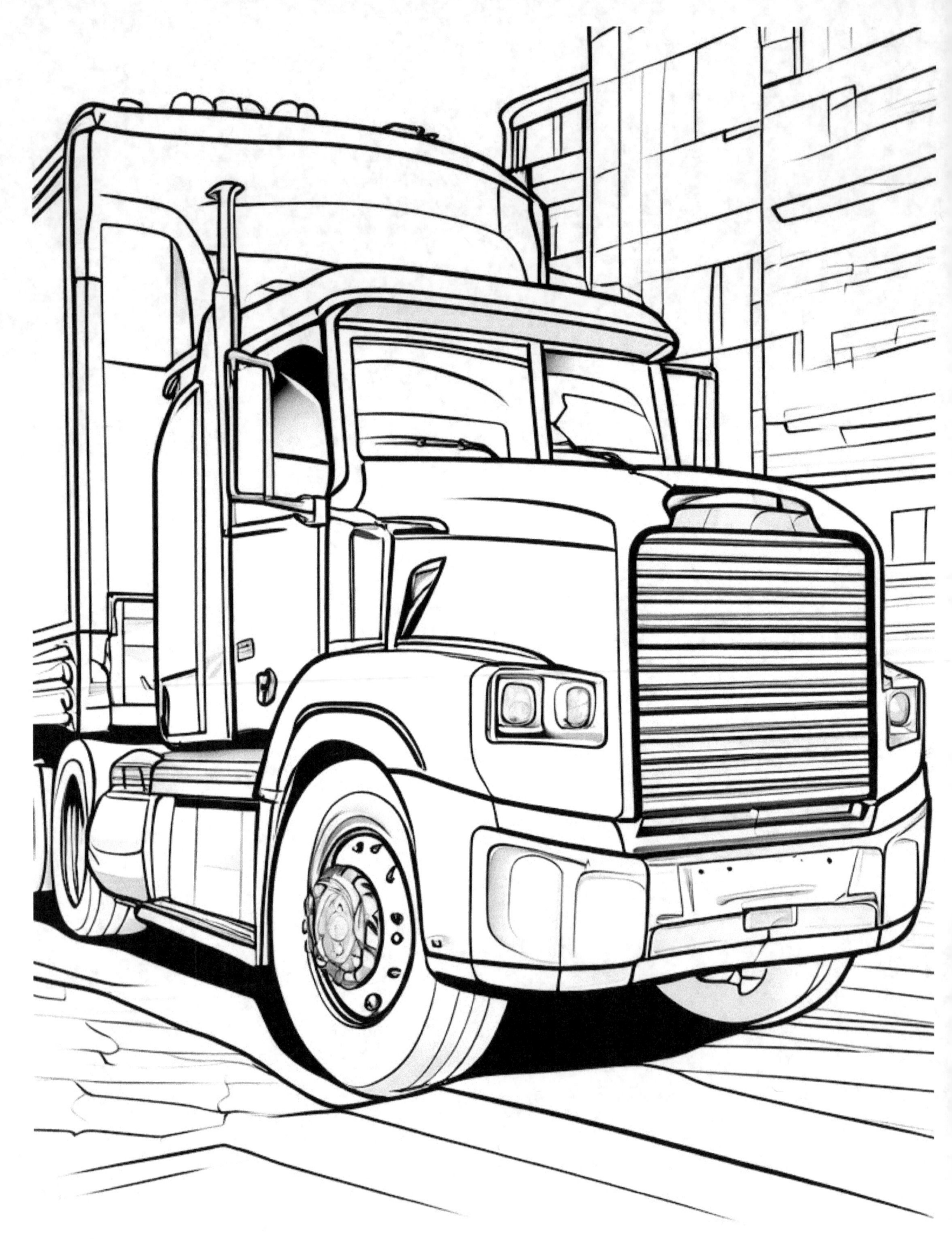

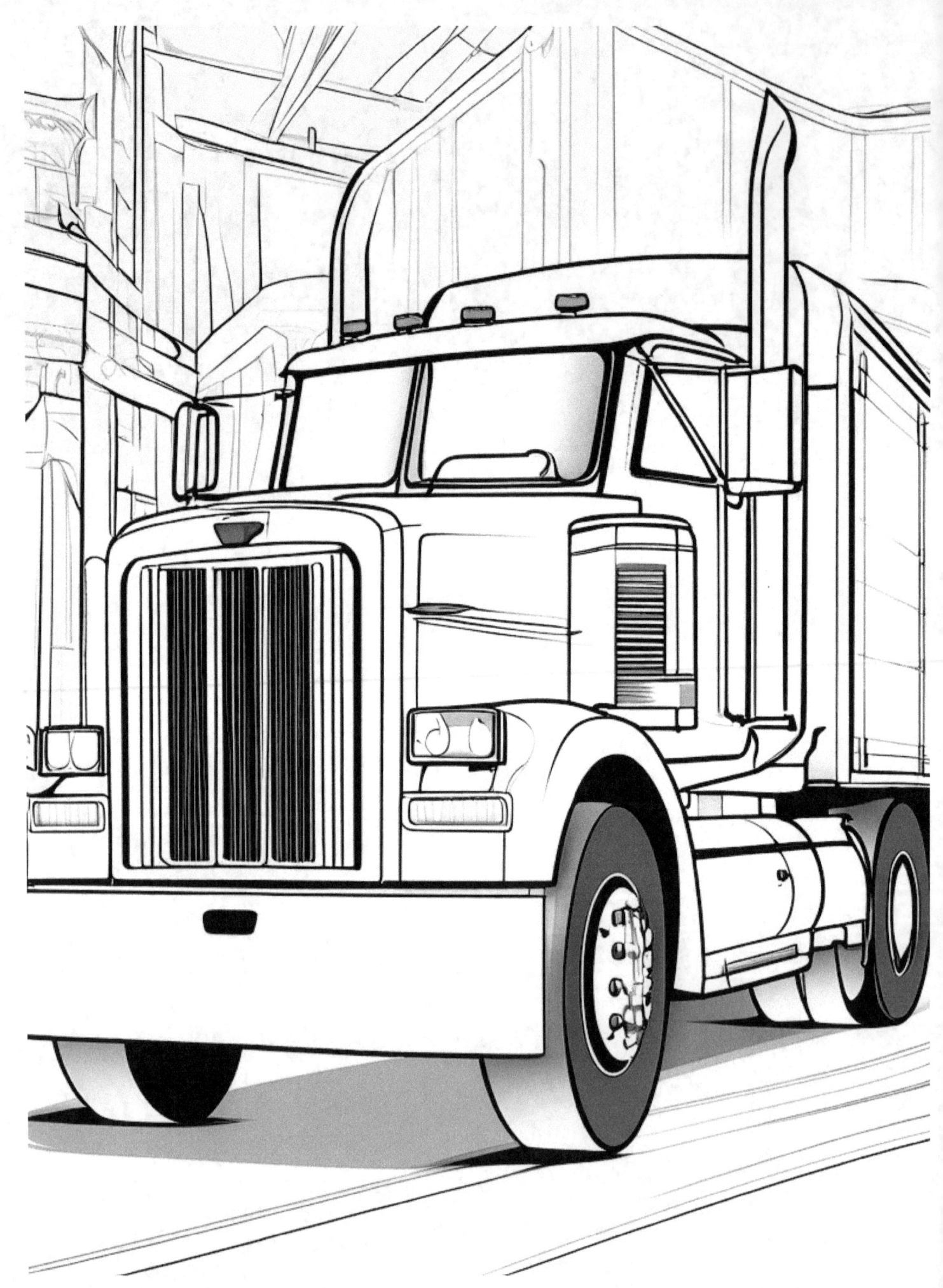

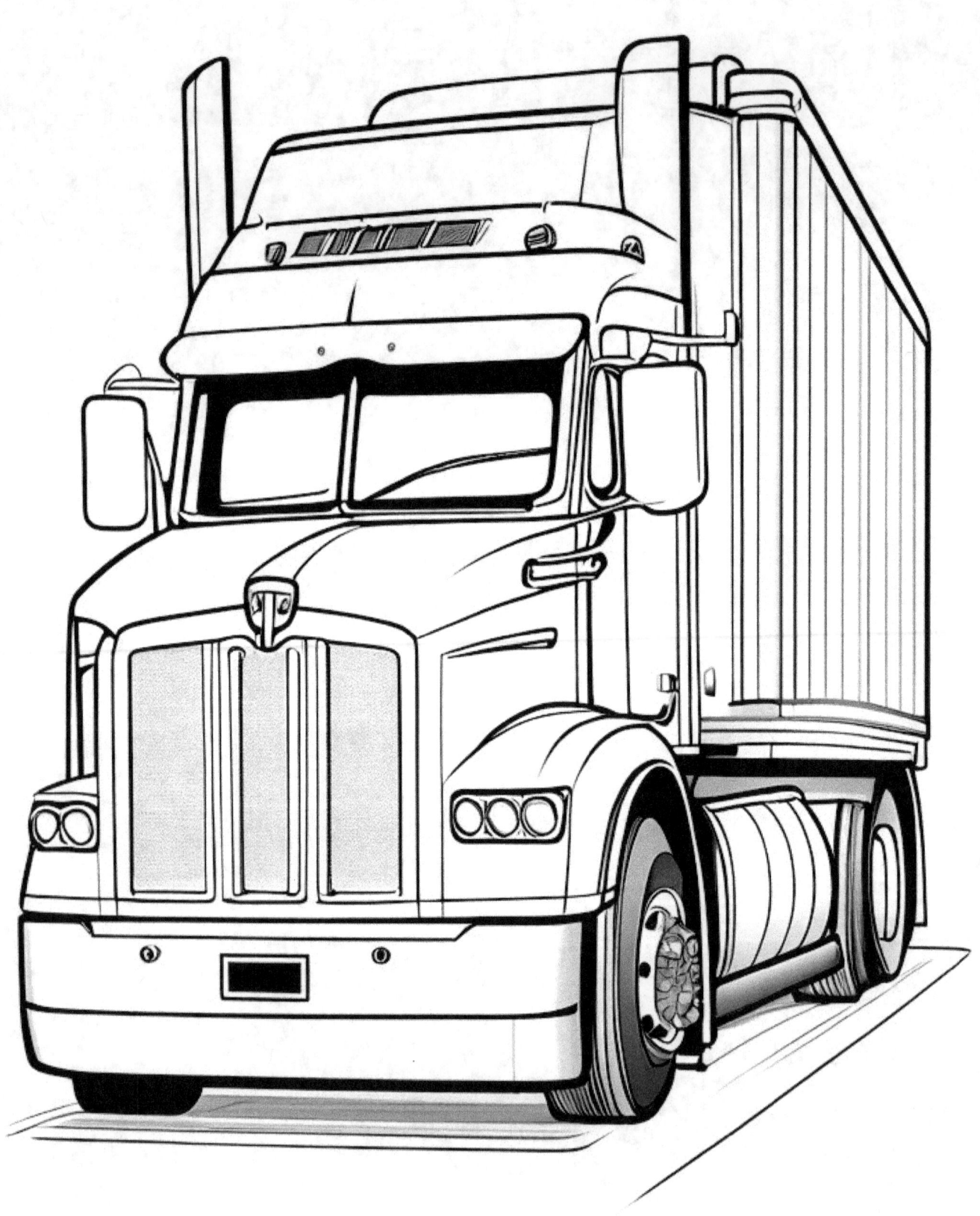

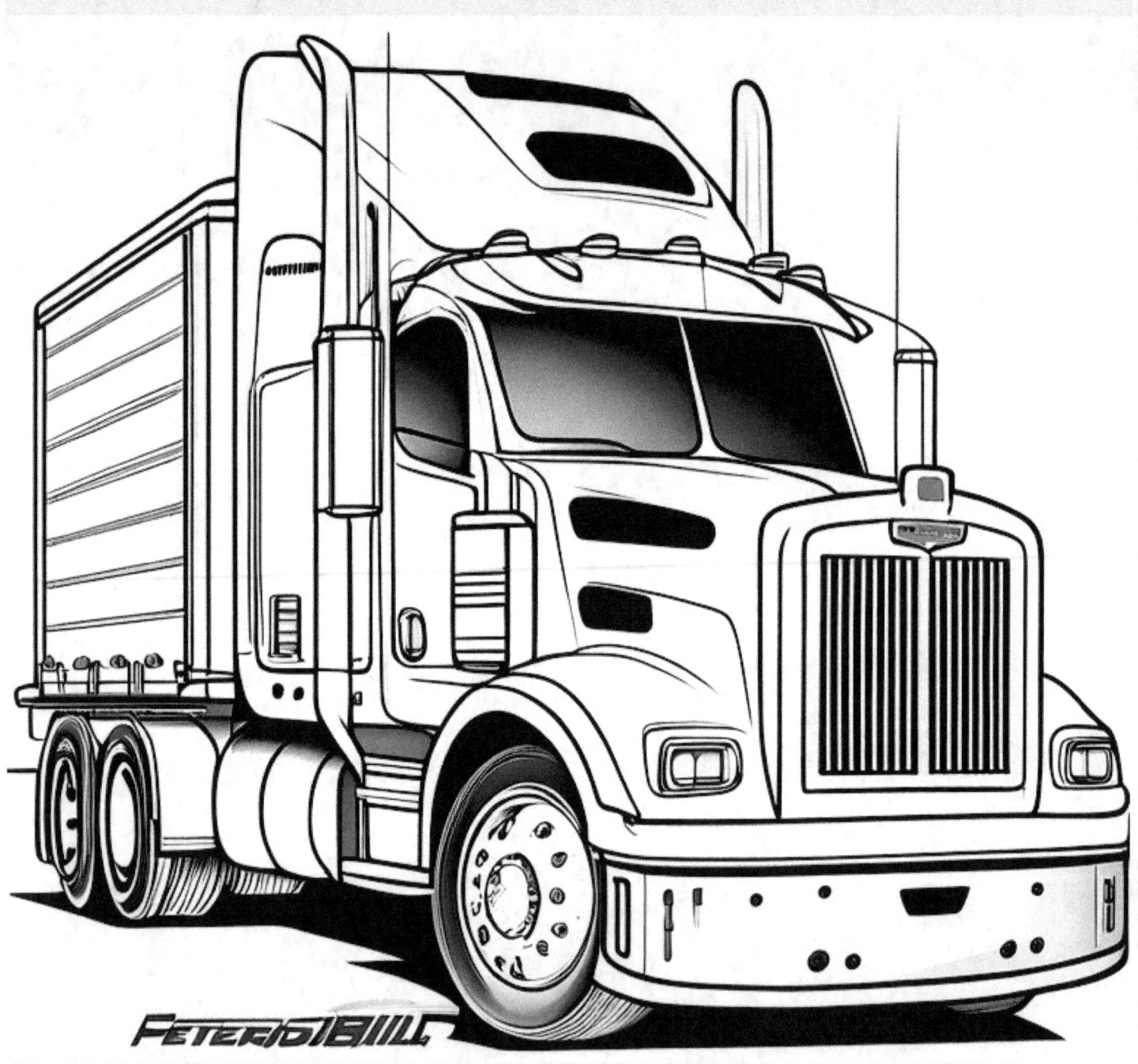

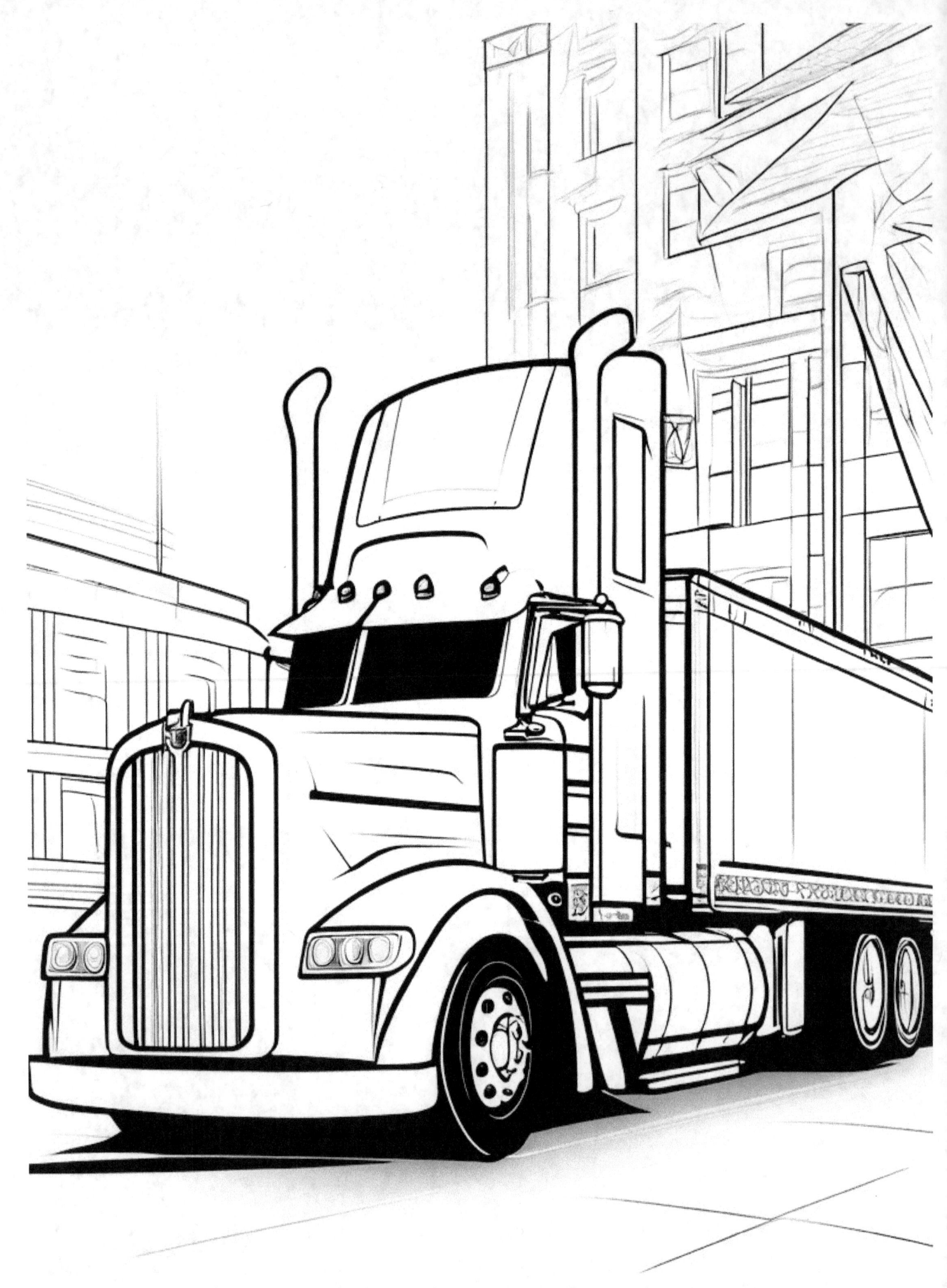

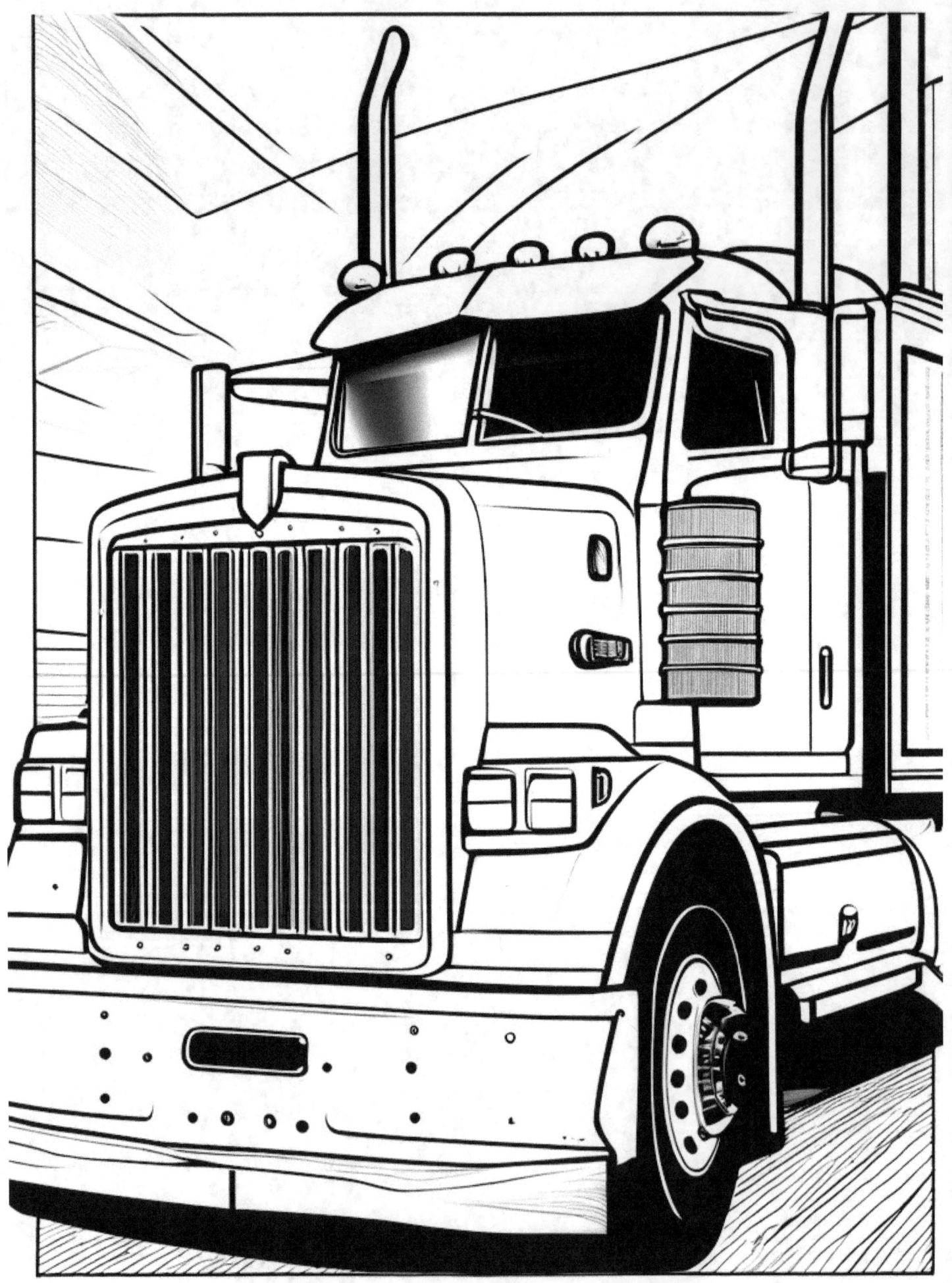

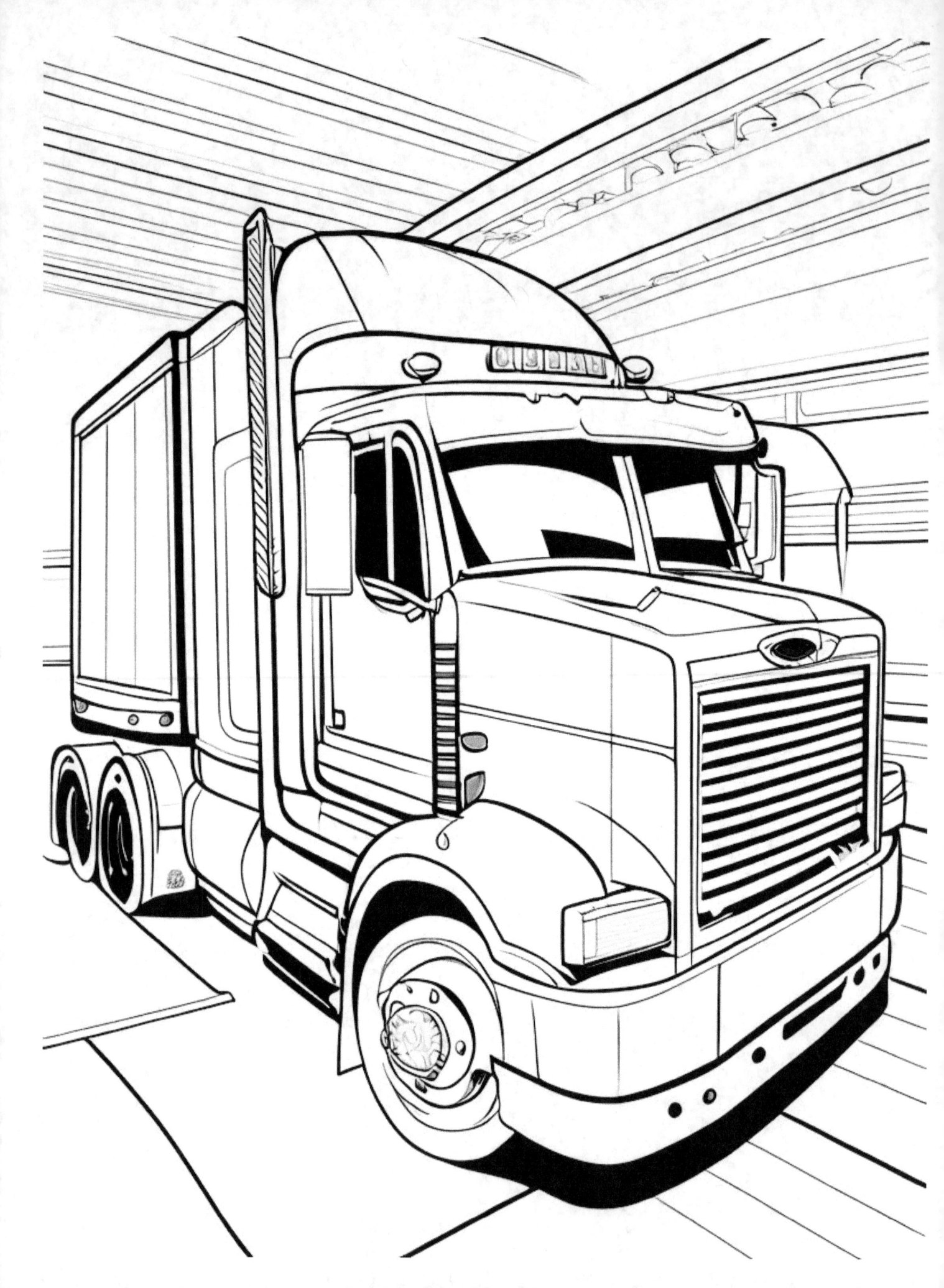

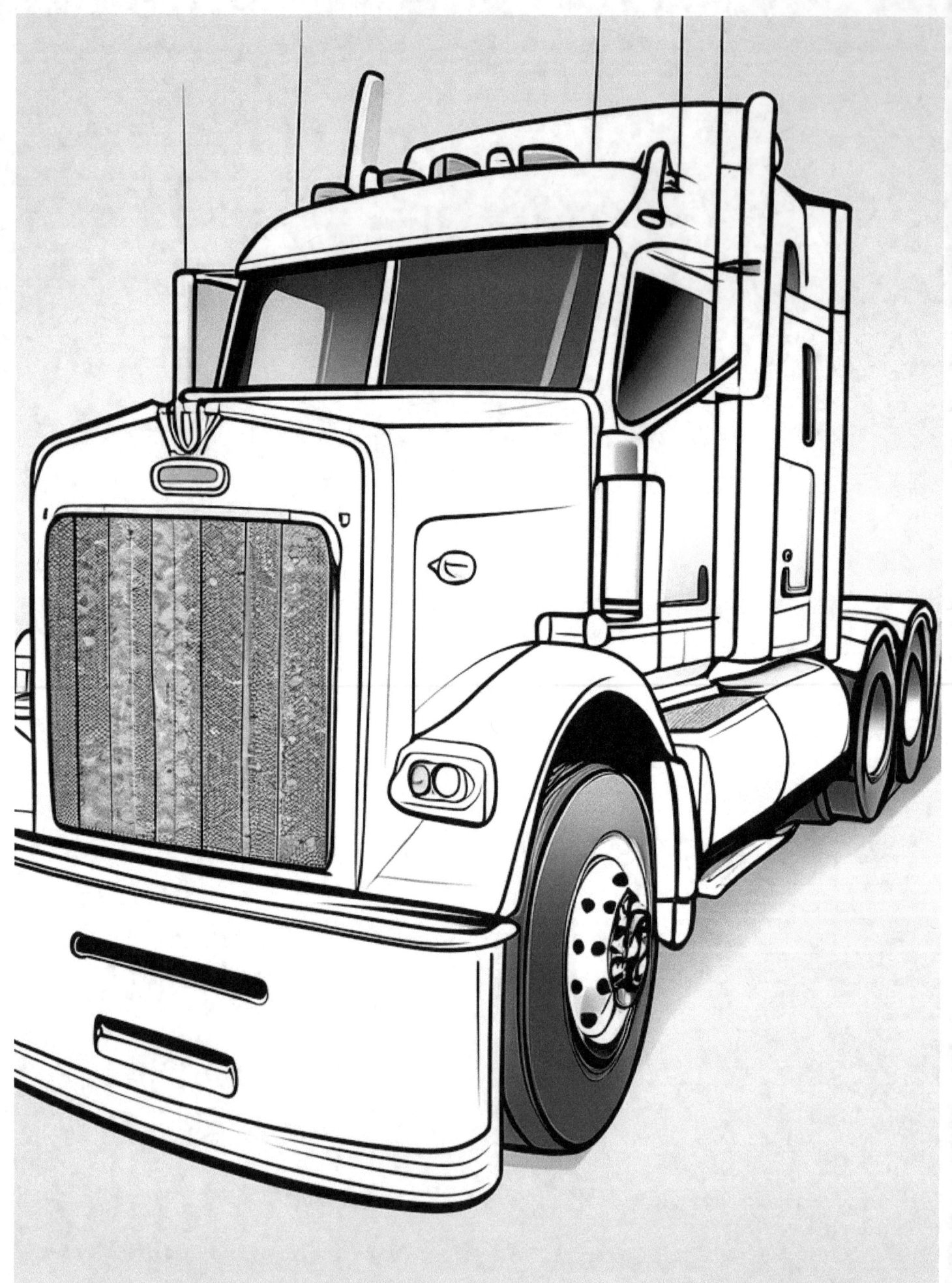

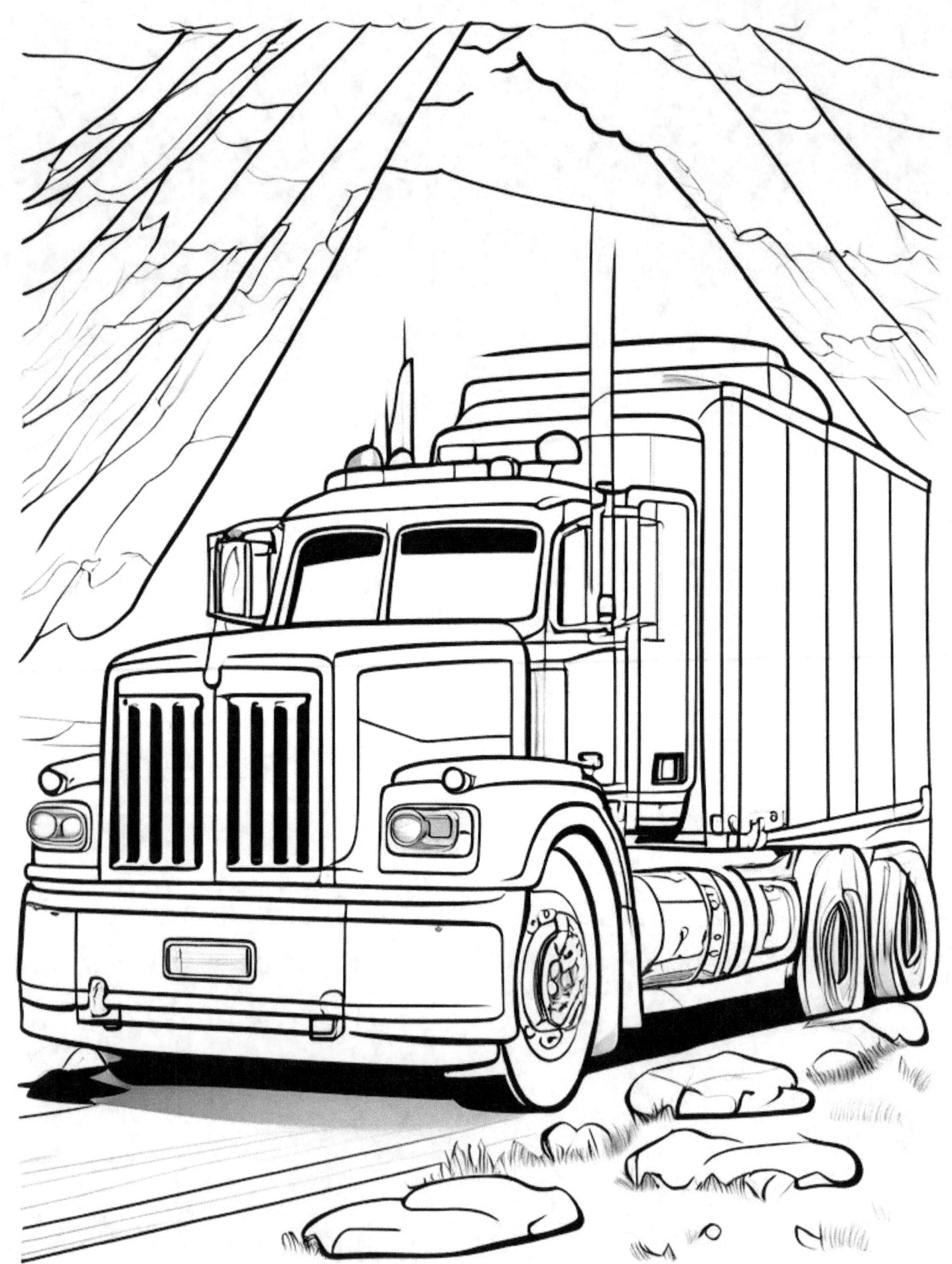

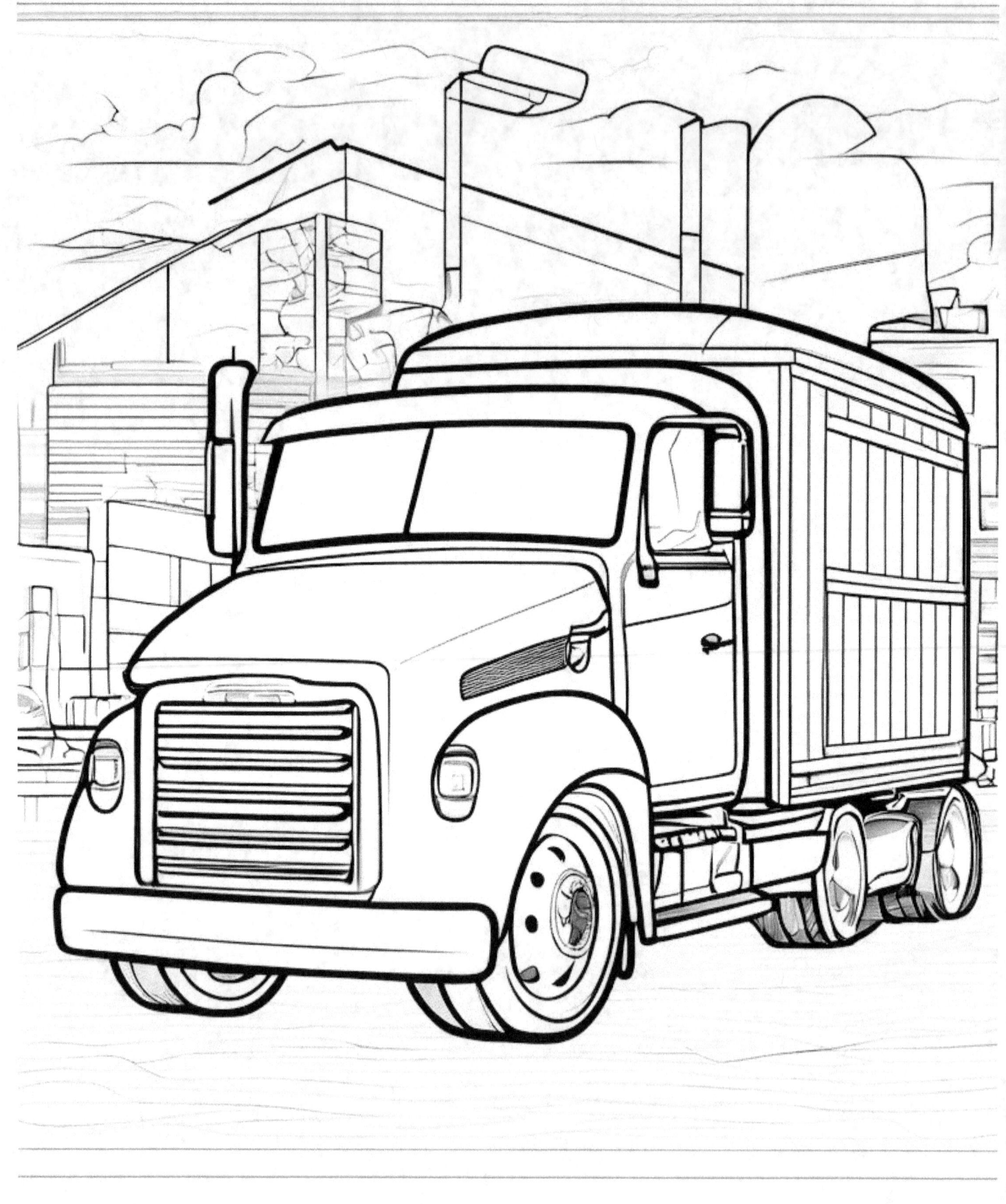

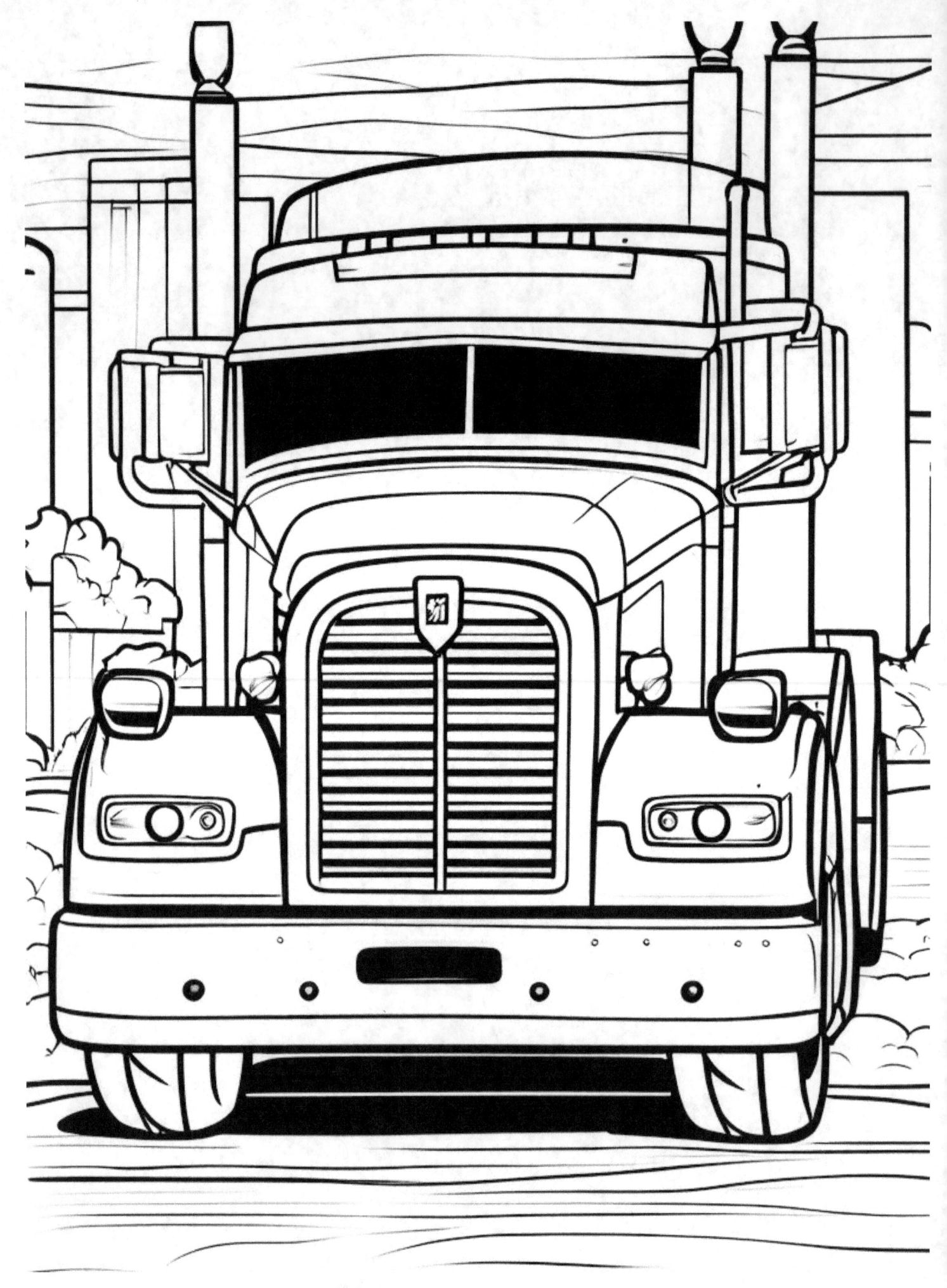

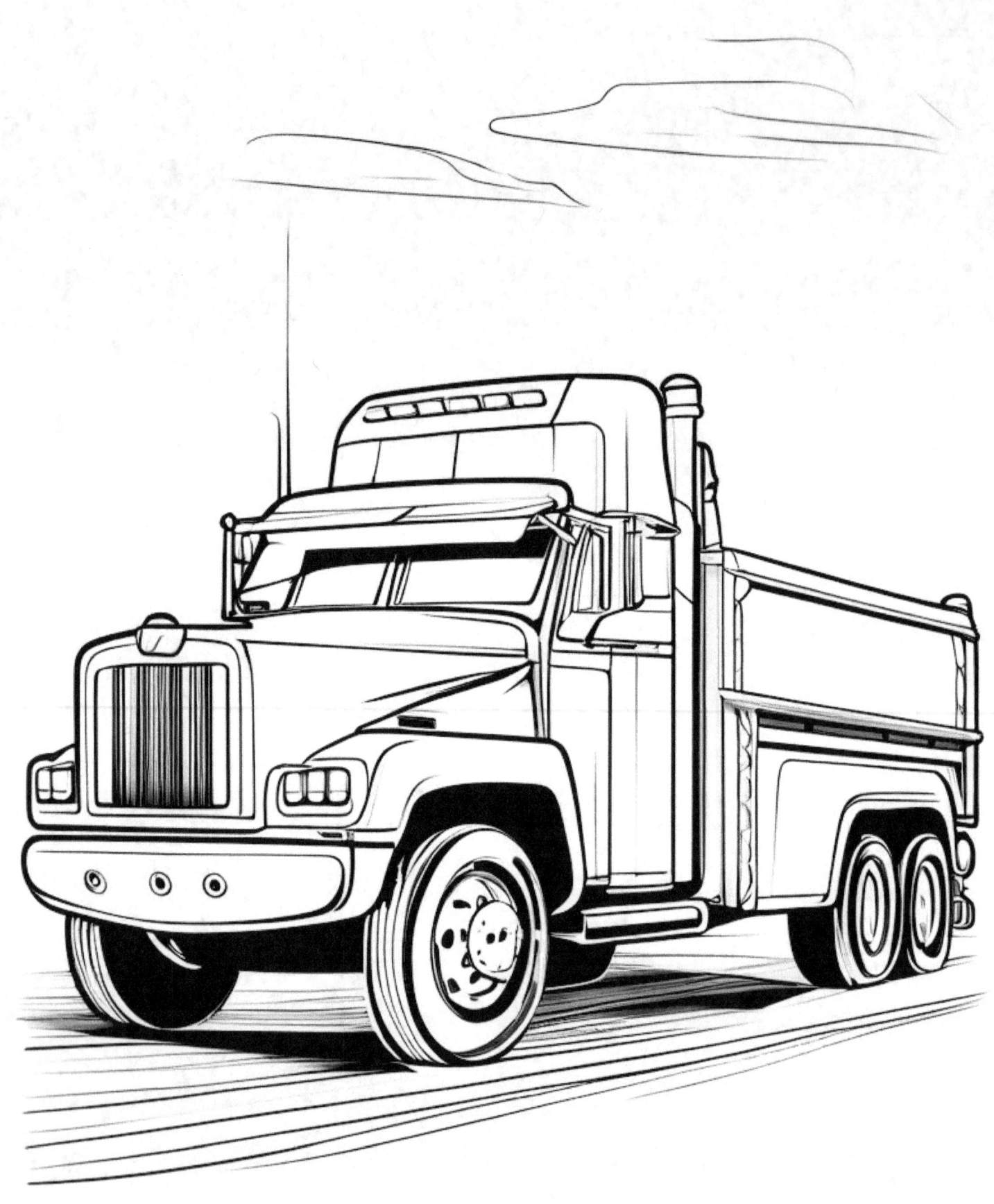

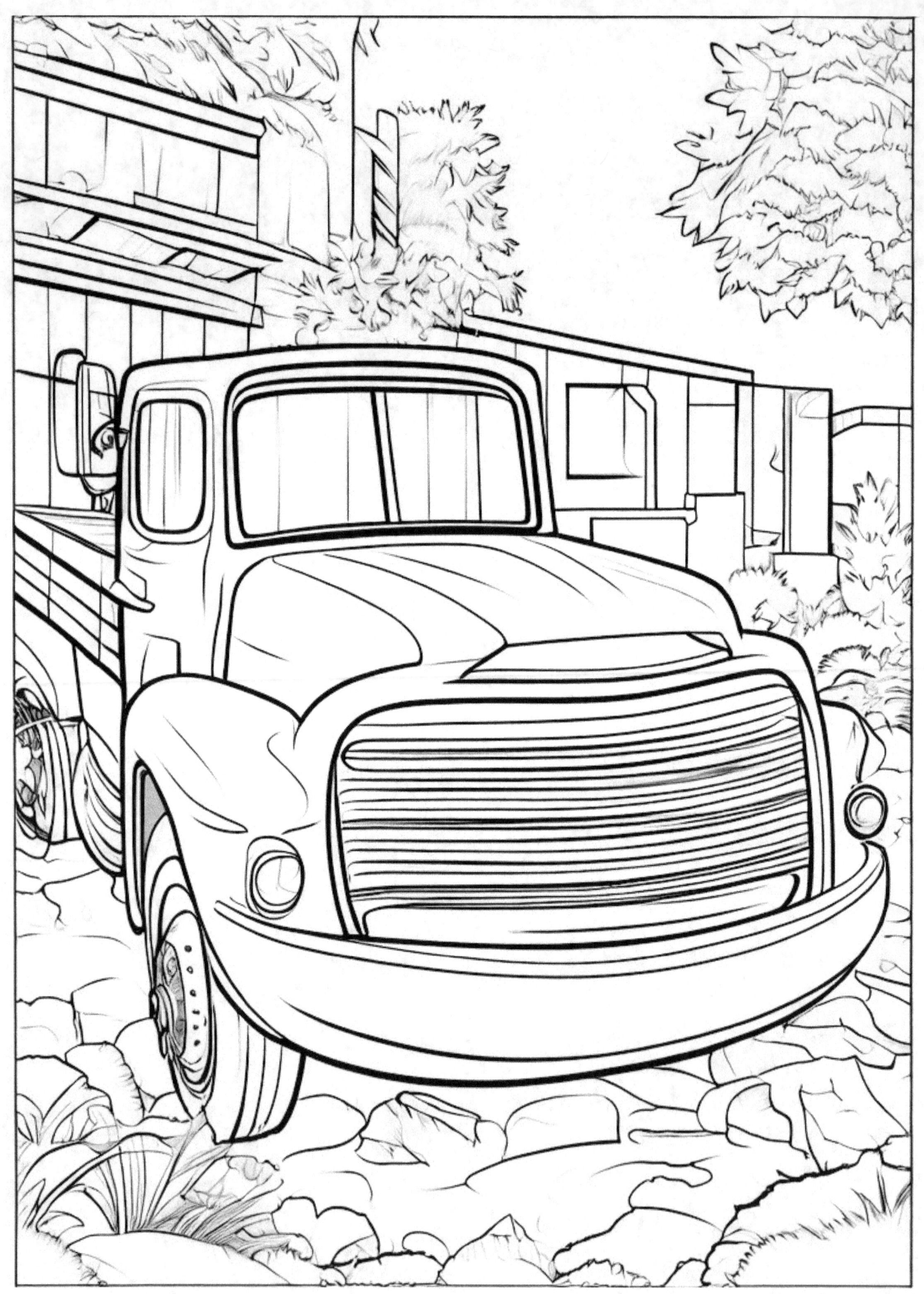

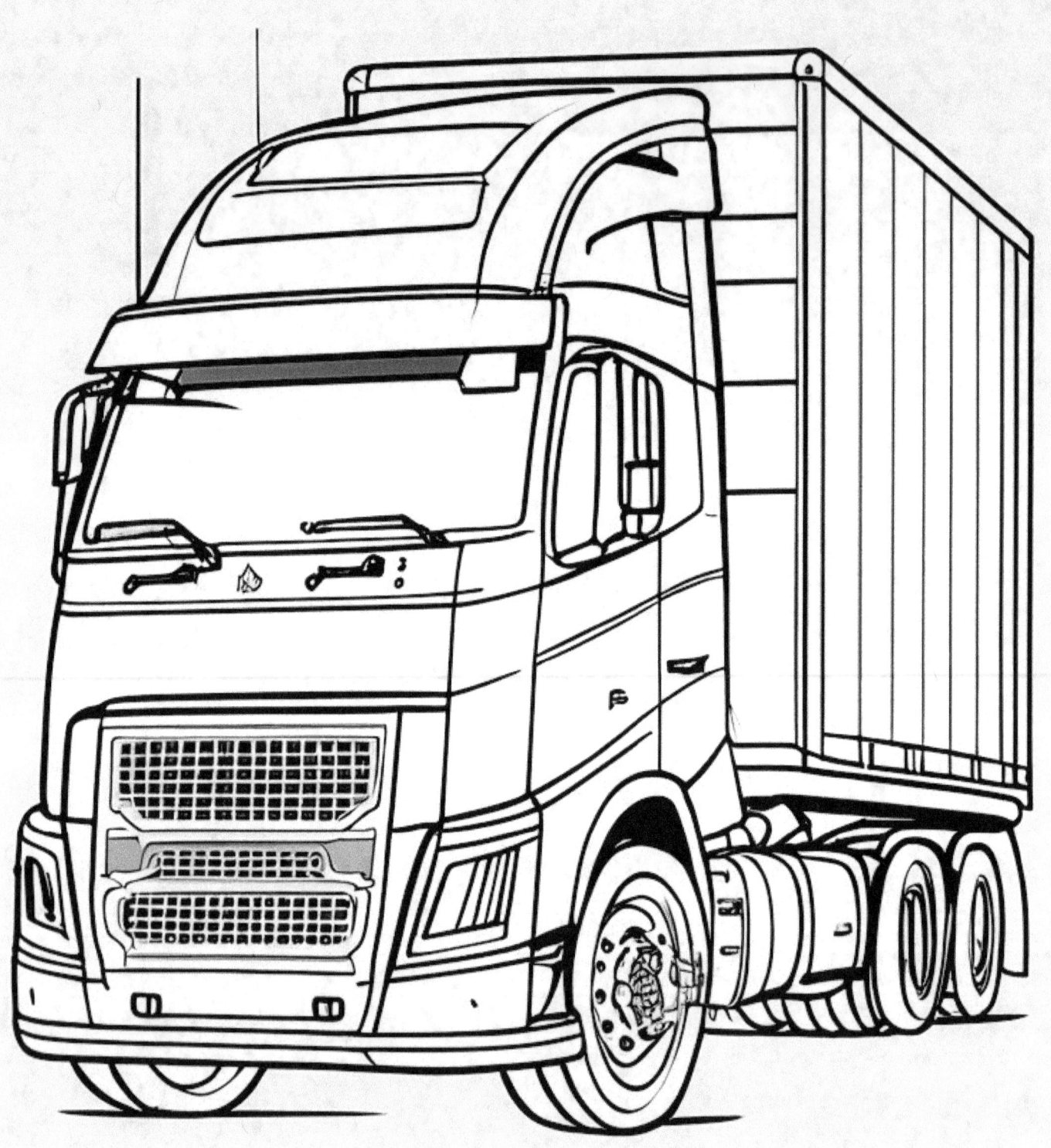

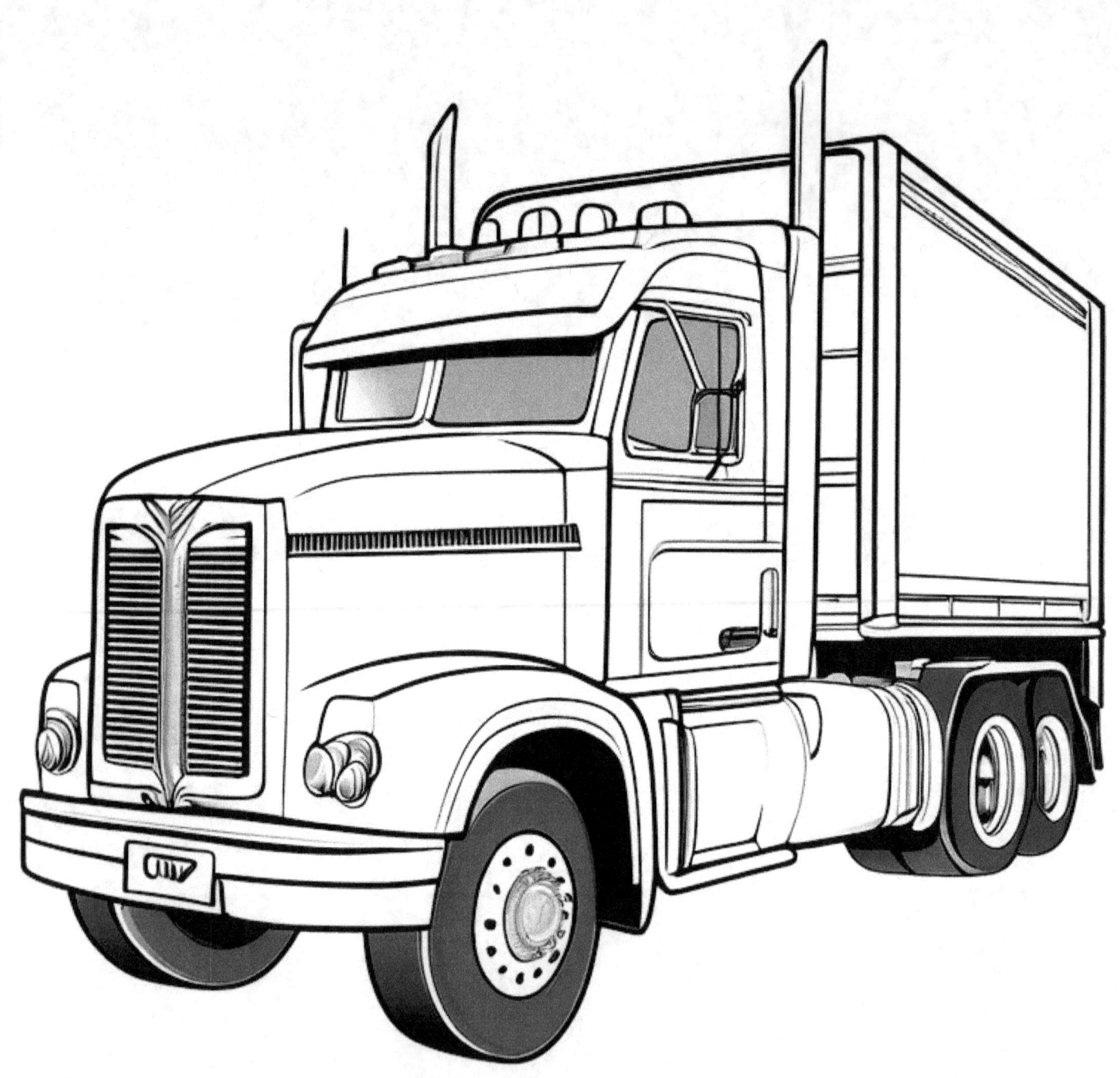

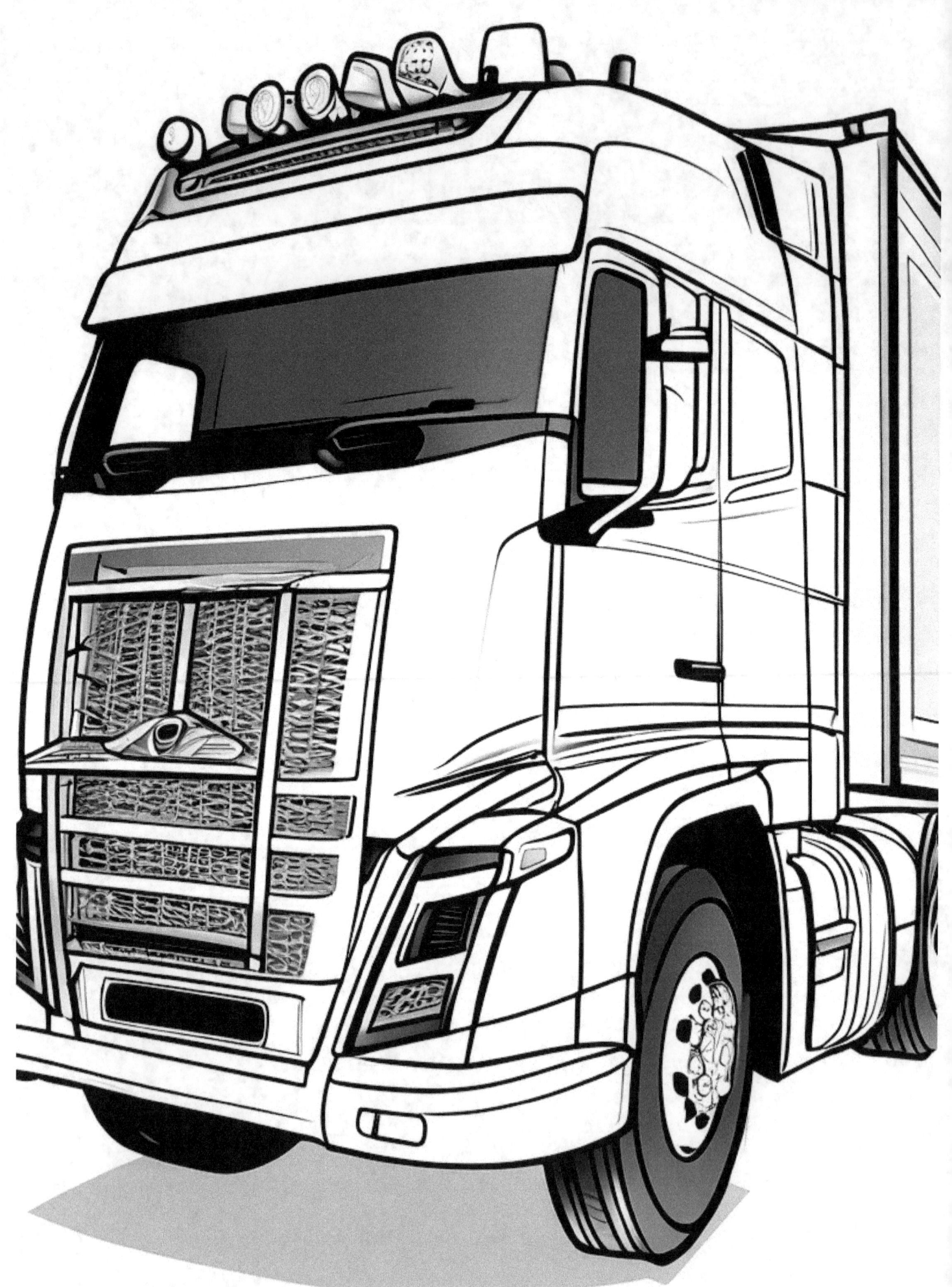

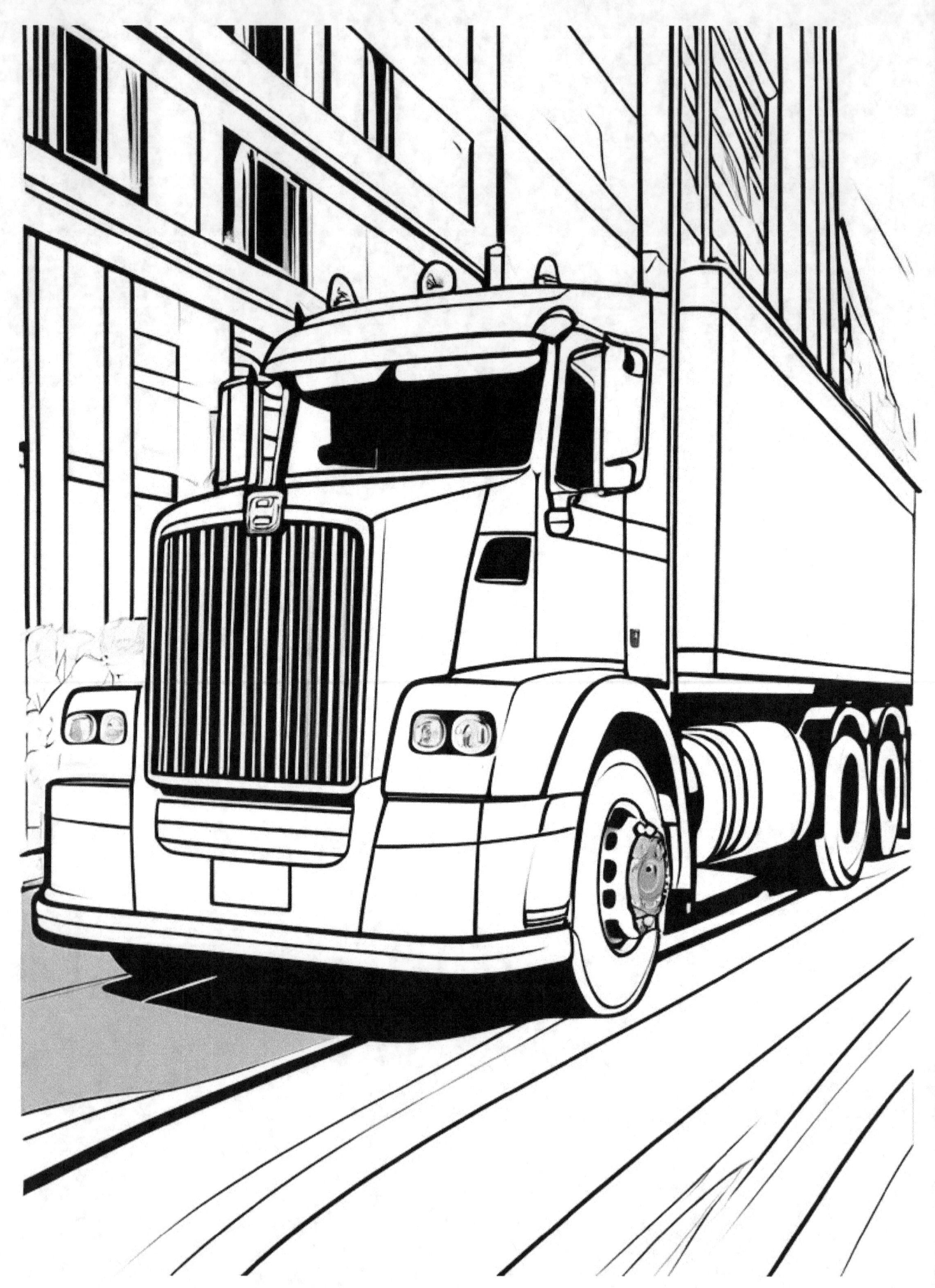

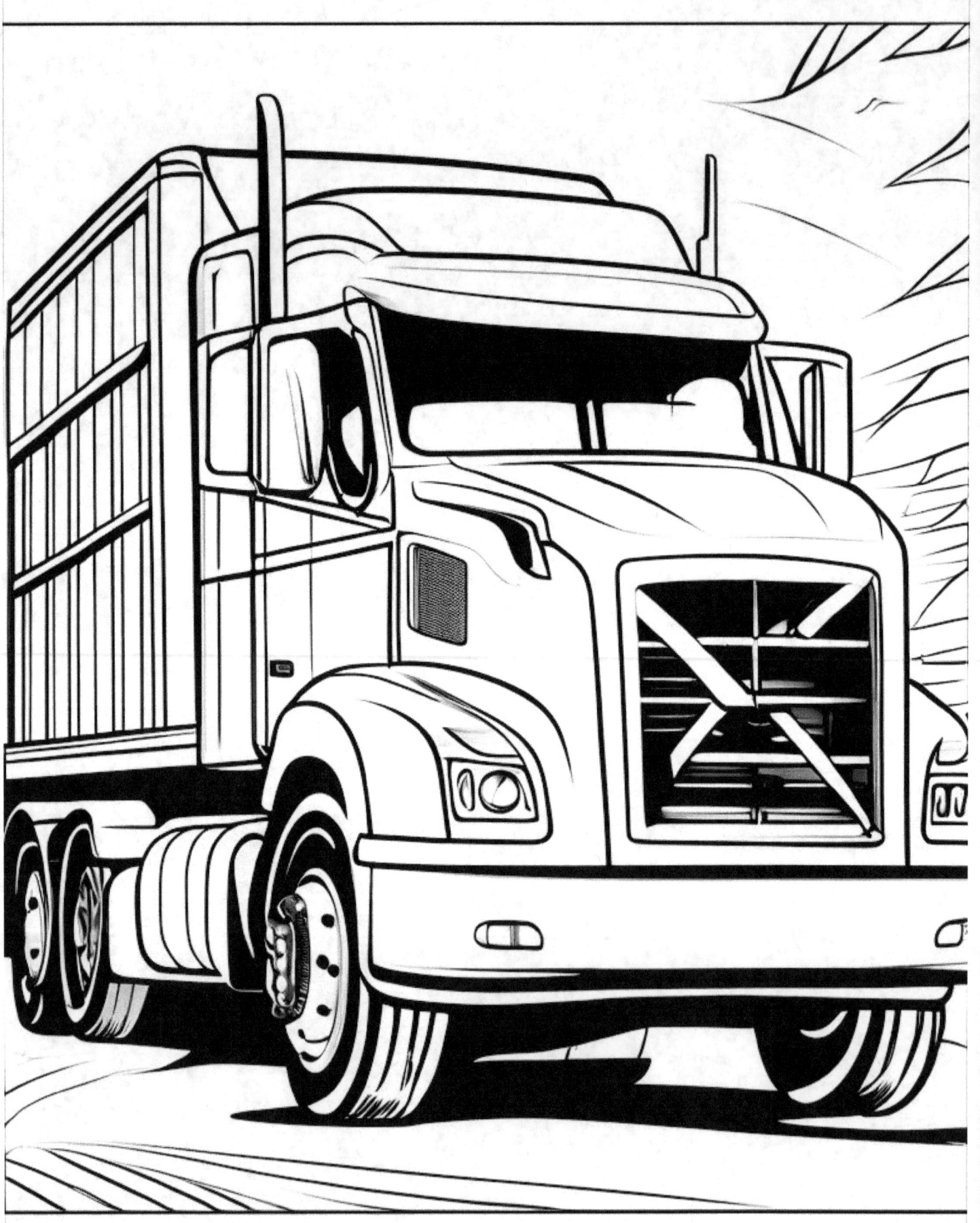

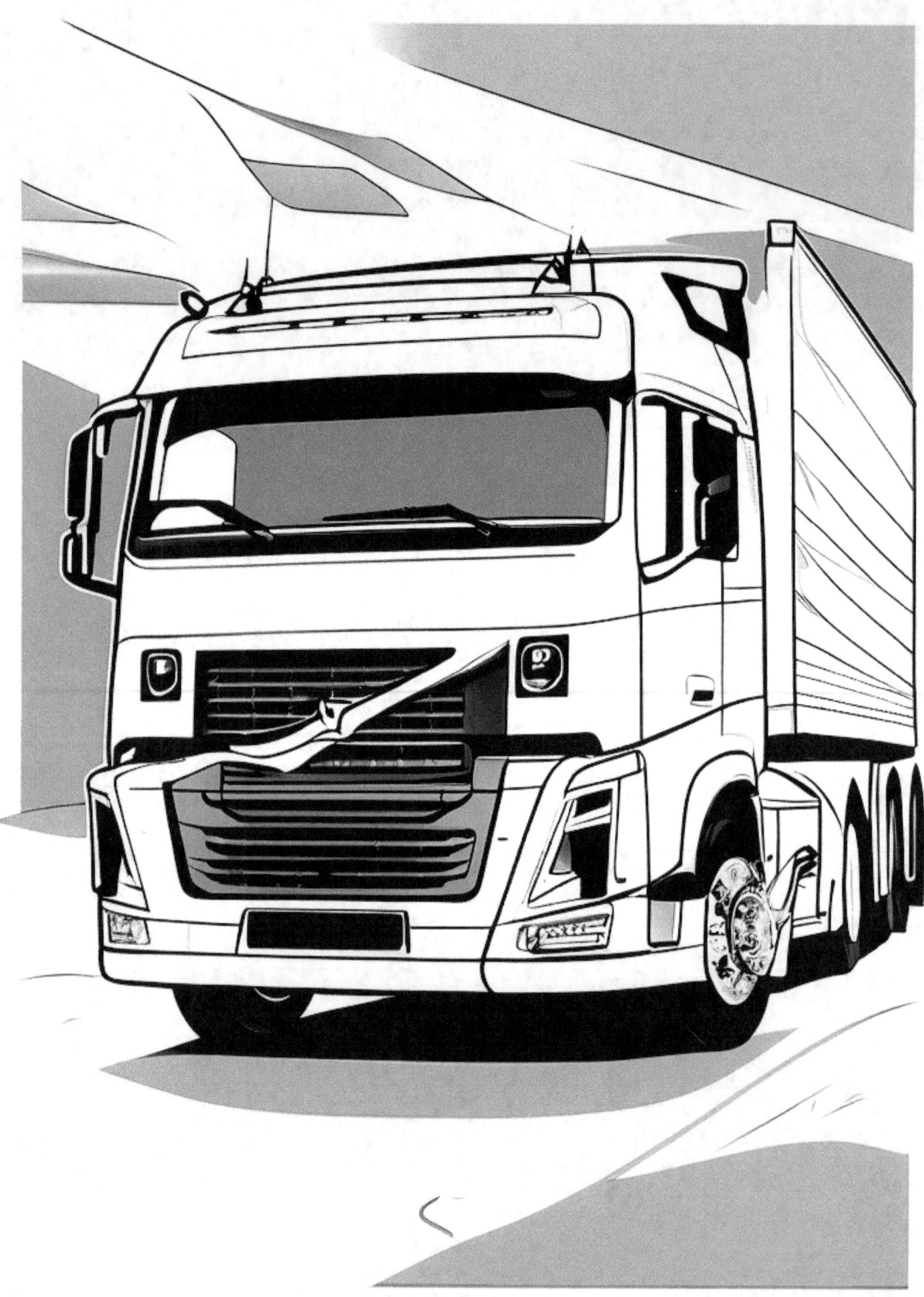

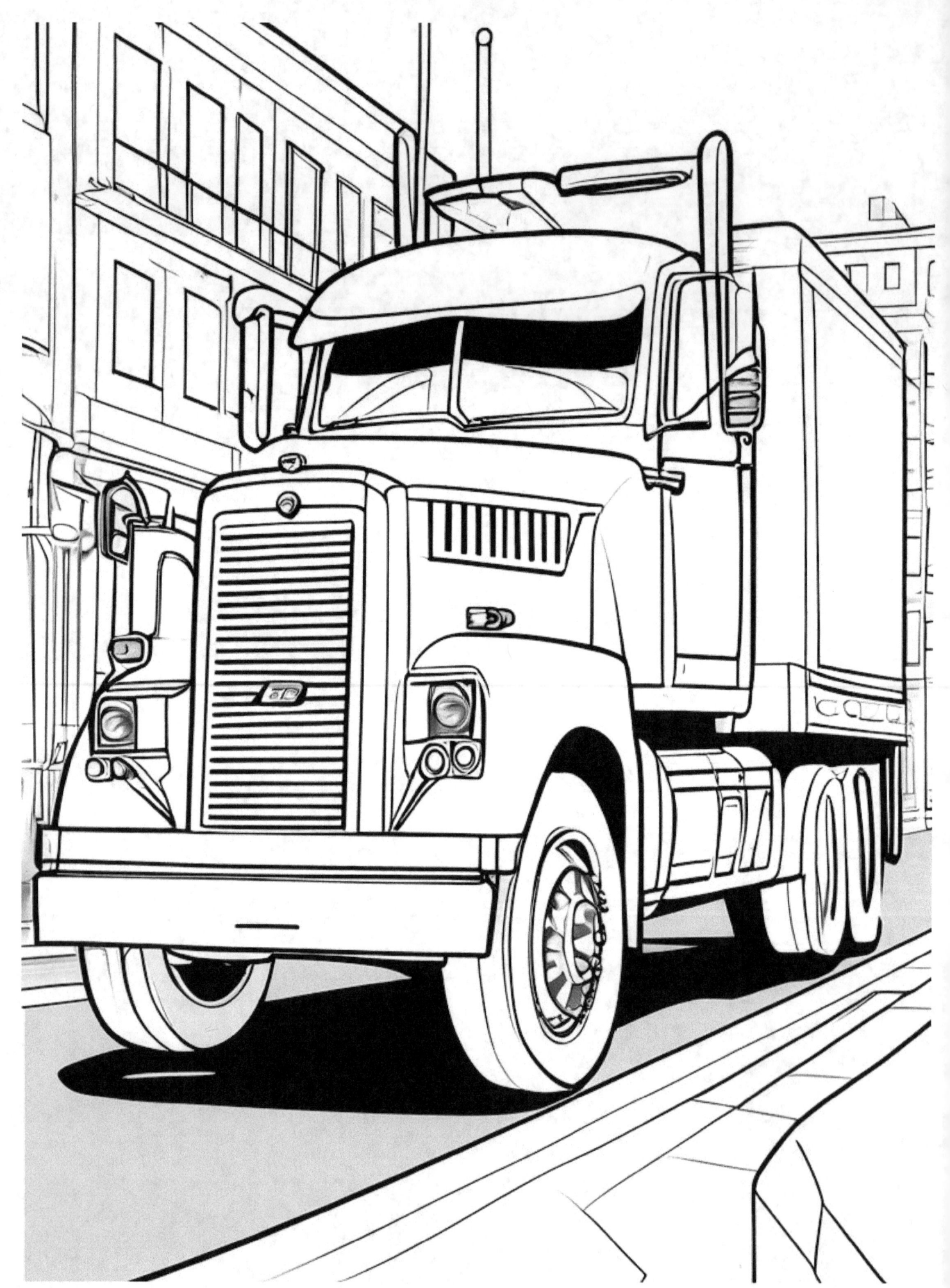

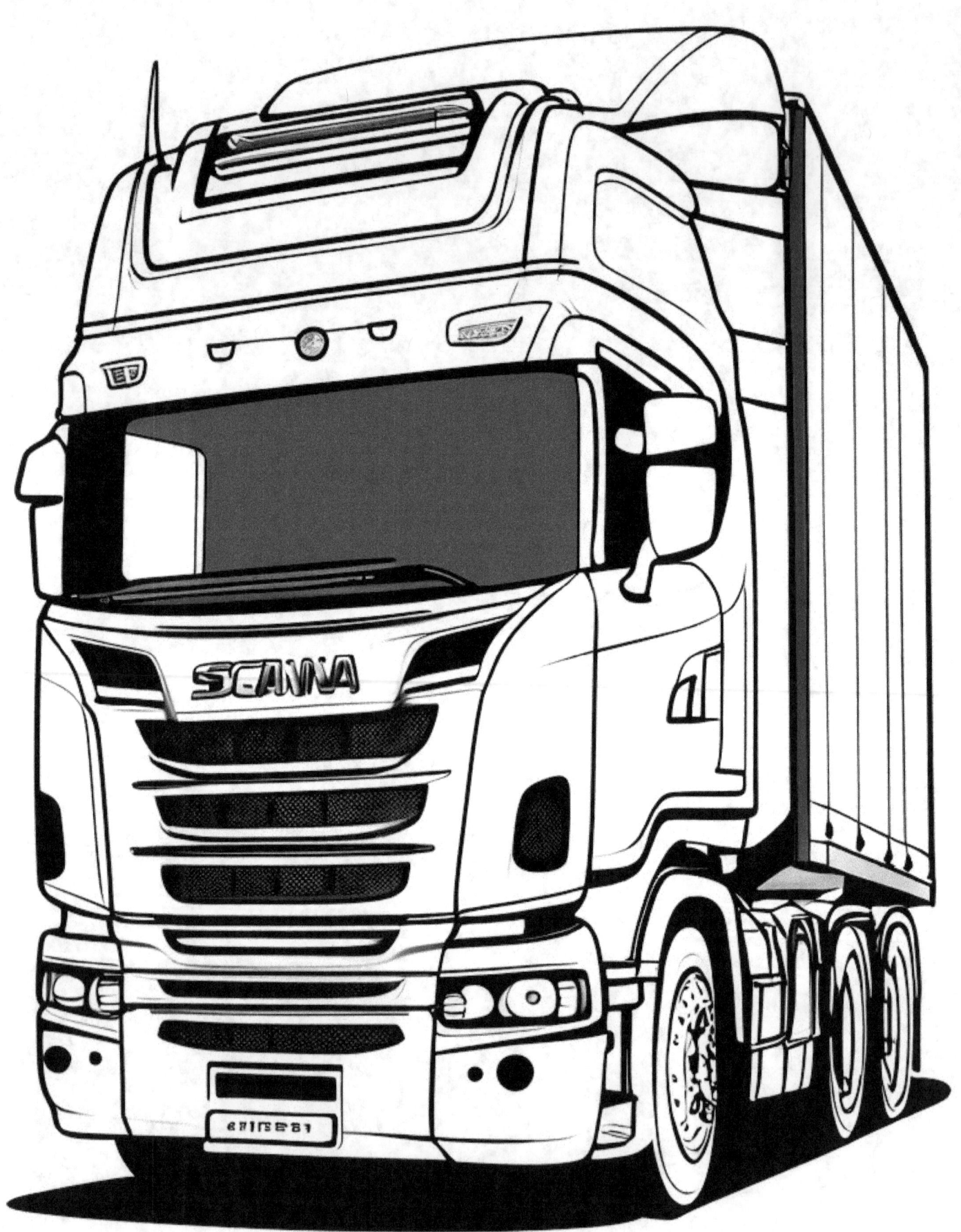

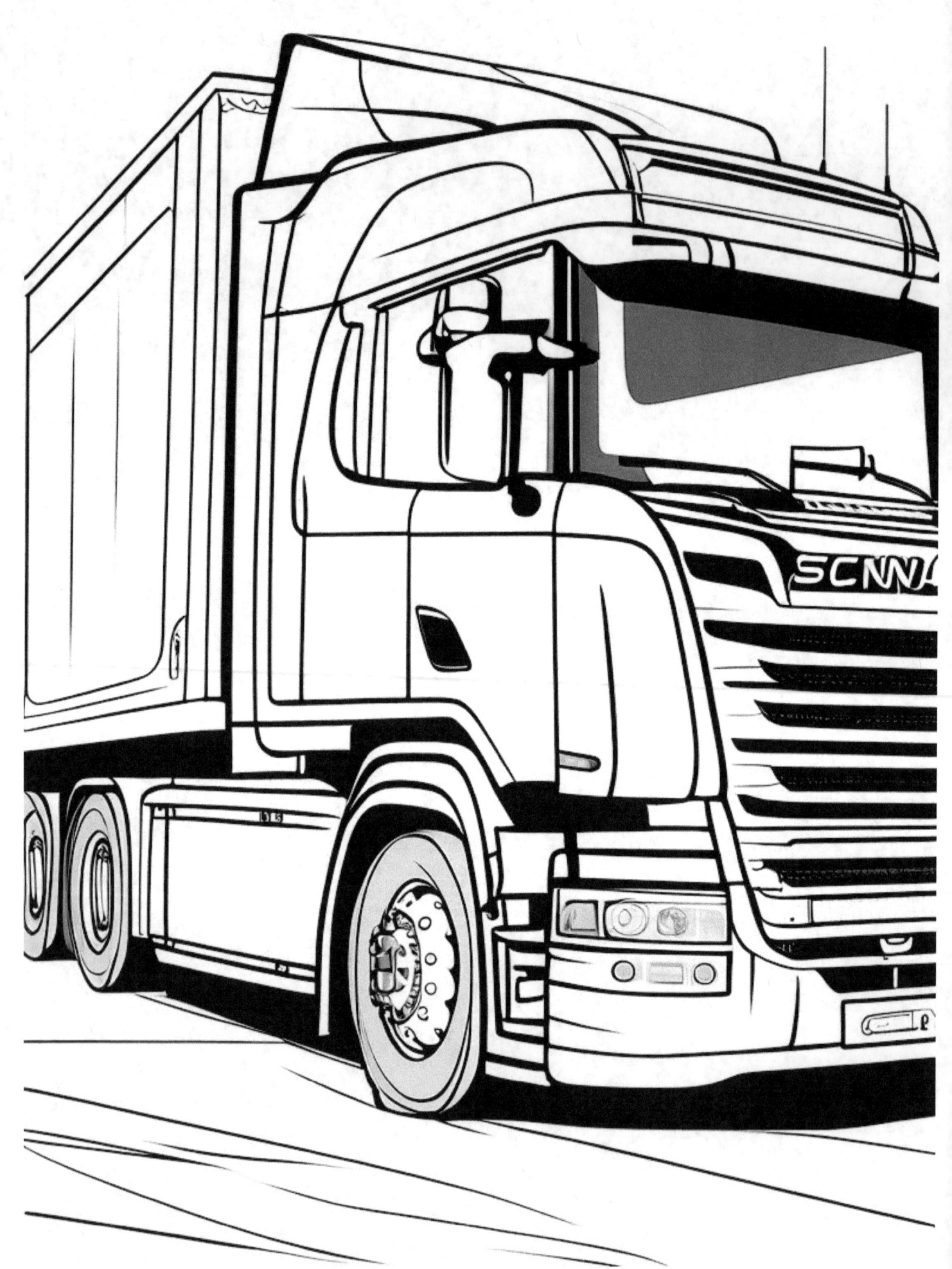

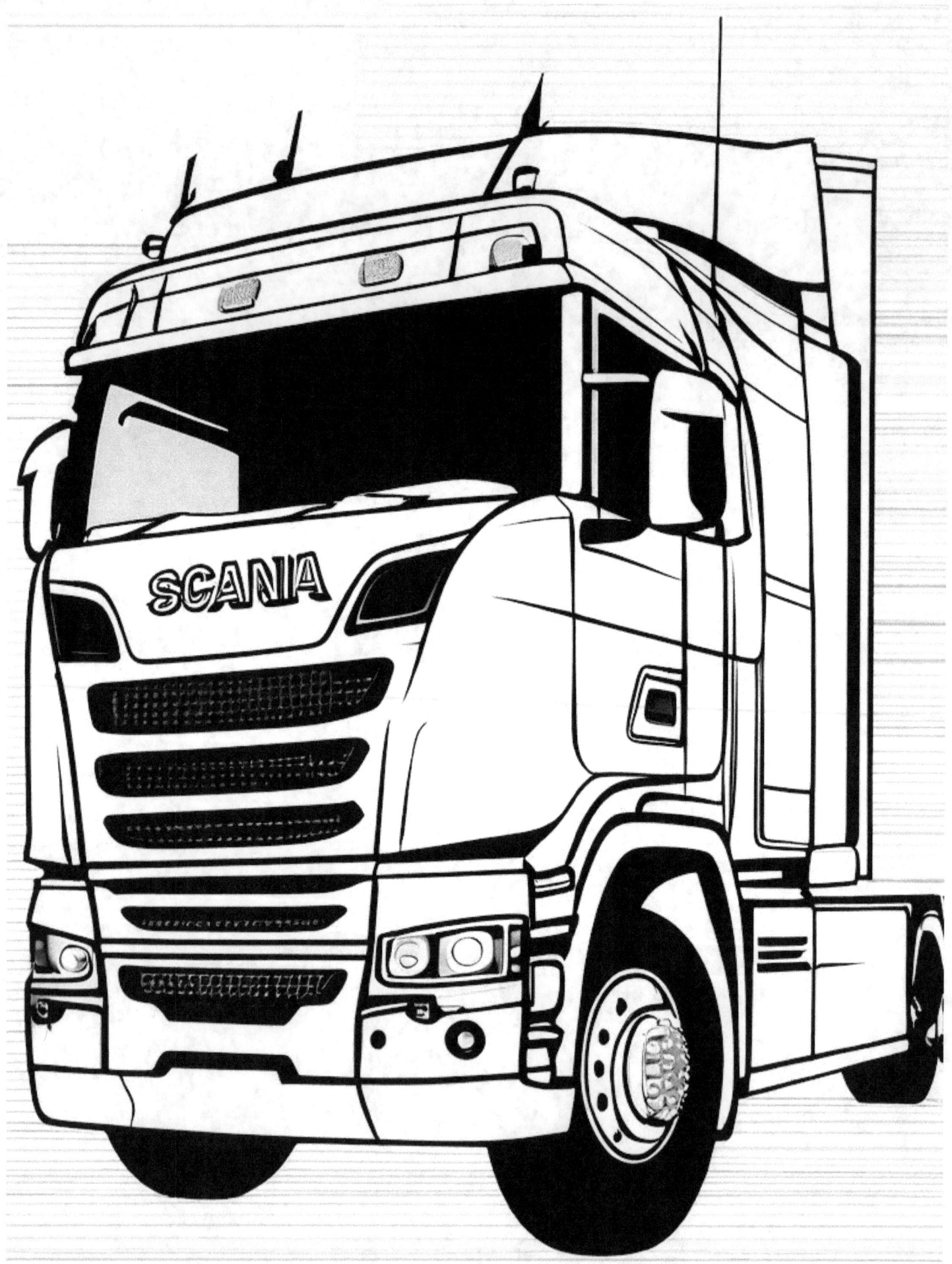

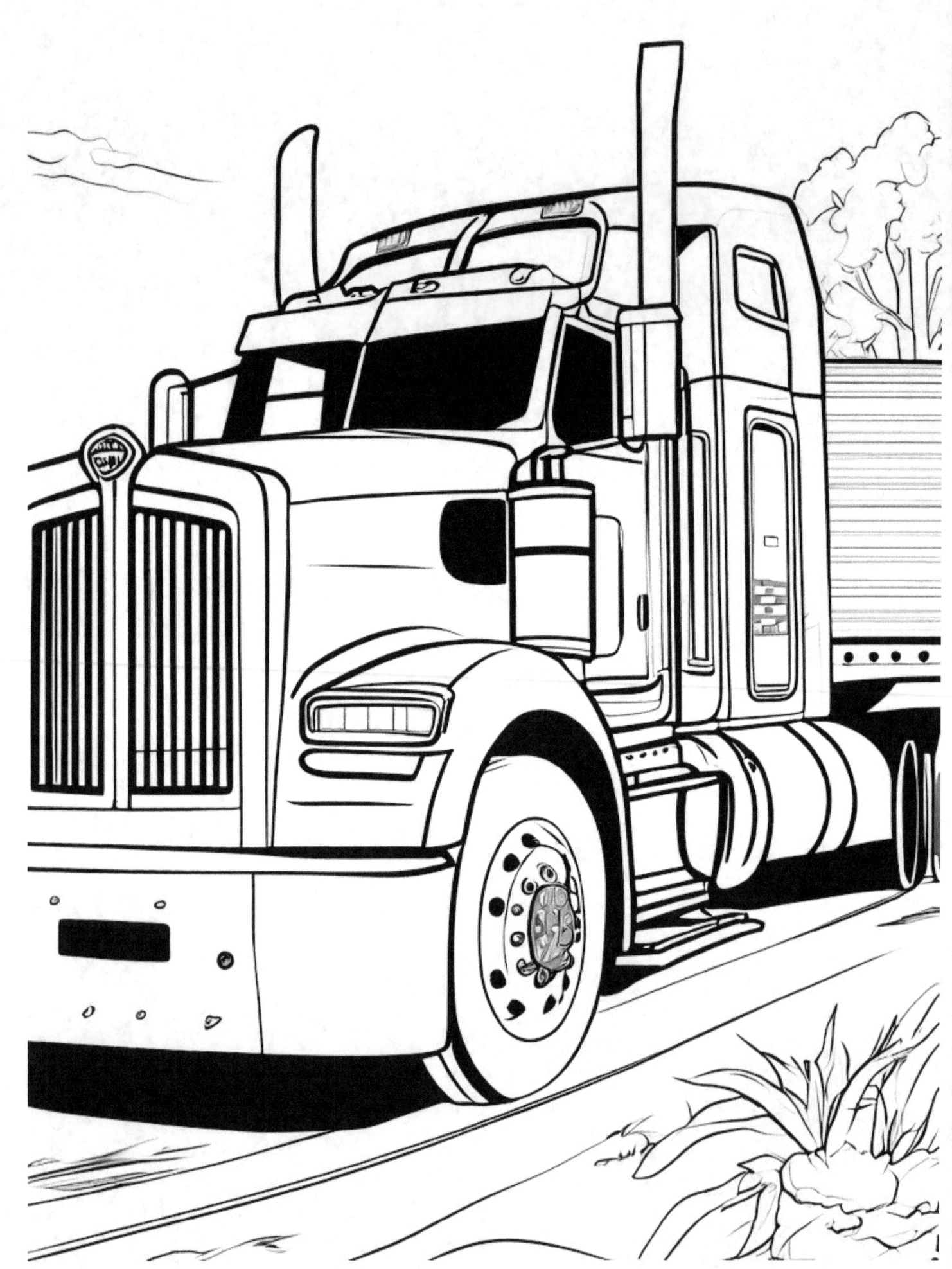

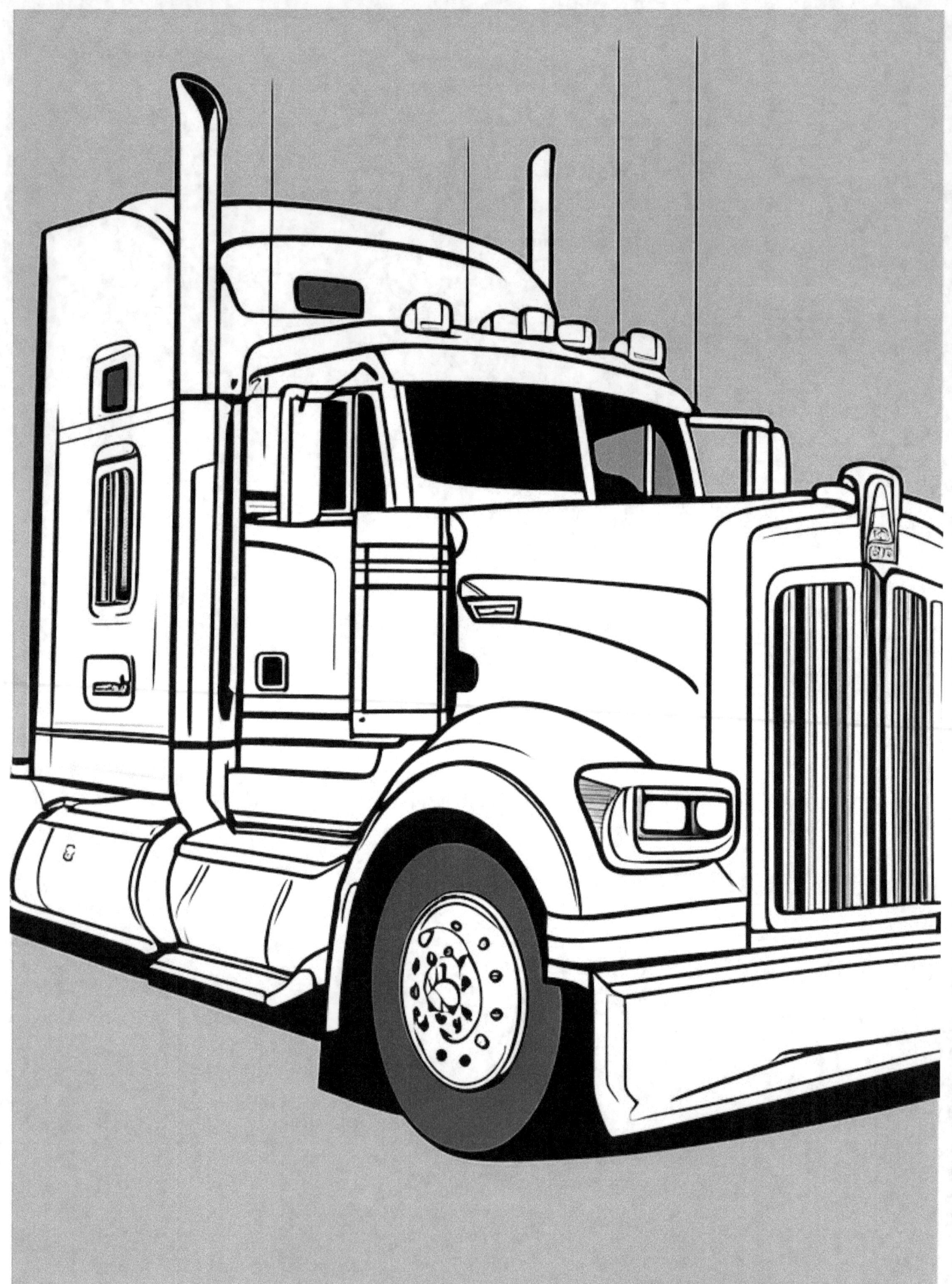

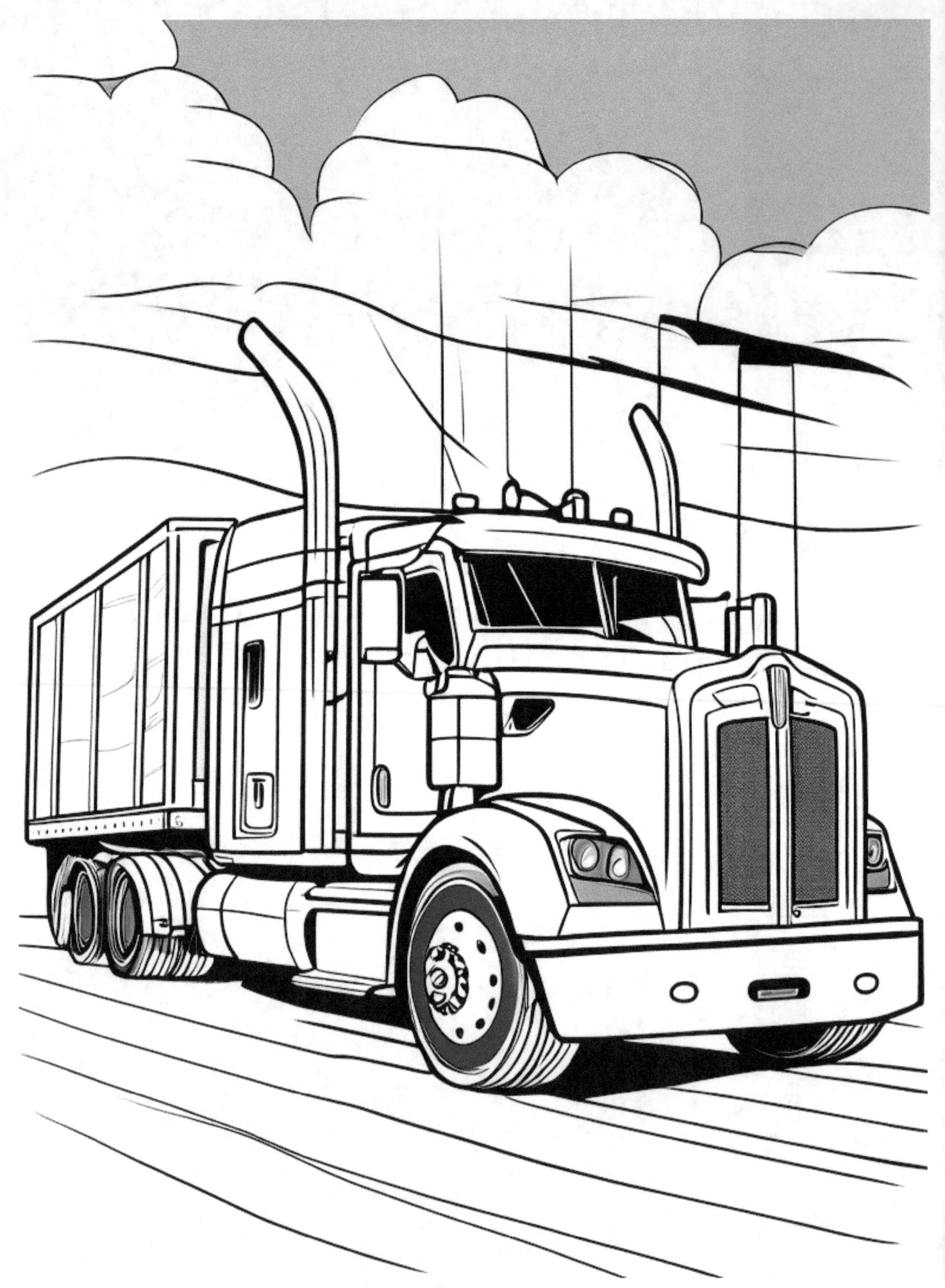

www.ingramcontent.com/pod-product-compliance
Lightning Source LLC
Chambersburg PA
CBHW062119220526
45471CB00010B/3798